Words From My Heart

by Amos Pinnock

Words From My Heart: Amos Pinnock

Non-Fiction Memoir

Copyright © 2017: Amos Pinnock
Published by Conscious Dreams Publishing

All rights reserved. This book or any portion thereof may not be reproduced or used in any manner whatsoever without the express written permission of the publisher except for the use of brief quotations in a book review.

Printed in the United Kingdom

First Printing 2017. Conscious Dreams Publishing.

All names and places have been changed to protect individuals concerned.

ISBN: 978-0-9955712-3-5

Publishing Company: www.consciousdreamspublishing.com

Contents

1st Letter 1
    The Start of Our Beginning 2
    Love in the Moment 3
    I Am Grateful 4
    At First Sight 5
    Goodbye to Goodbyes 6
    Selfish 8
    Walls of Your Emotions 9
    Trust My Love 10
    Is It Just Me 11
    In My Arms 13
    A Love for All to See 14
    I Hate Our Distance 15
    Phone Calls 16
    Hate that I Love You 18
    Show Me Your Love 19
    Just a Memory 20

2nd Letter 22
    I Want to Strip Your Heart 23
    Investment of Love 24
    I Feel Your Pain 25
    I Can't Help But Miss You 26
    We Had to Stop Talking 28
    Her Apology for My Pain 29
    Never Going Back 30
    Oh Girl 32
    Let Me Fall in Love with You 33

I Won't Wait I'll You're Gone to Love You 34
The Beautiful Switch 36
Shy Around You 37

3rd Letter **39**
Always and Forever 40
Young Hearts 41
A Truthful Lie 43
A Life Sentence 44
Loneliness is Lonely 46
You Can Tell Me Anything 47
You Make Me Happy 49
Random Thought 50
Black Heart 52
Just a Reminder 53
I Wish We Could Have Been 54

4th Letter **56**
My Destiny 57
A True Imagination 58
Walking Without Friendship 59
Love 60
Protection 61
Cry 62
To You 64
The Beauty of Your Mind 65
The Day We Meet 66
I'm Doing My Part 68
You Get Me Mad 69

5th Letter **71**
Love with Faith 72

One Night 73
Crazy in Love 74
Trust Me to Love You 75
Snow Angel 77
Ezbie 78
You Next to Me 79
A Fight for Love 80
Girl You Deserve the Best 81
I'm Letting You Go so I Can Be Loved 83
A Consistent Love 84
I'm Happy to Love You 85
I Want to Hear From You 86

6th Letter **88**
Just Me and You 89
I'll See You Soon 90
Inside Love 91
A Wish and a Hate 93
The Pain of Distance 94
You Matter to Me 95

7th Letter **97**
My Miracle 98
Perfect Beauty 99
Story Behind a Tear 101
Heart Under Oath 102
I Can See You See Me 103
Exit Out My Heart 104
Know Your Worth 106
To My Mother 107
A Lookout 108

- Let's Make Us Happen 110
- I Want to Feel Loved Too 111
- A Real Goodbye 112
- Like It's Our Last Time 114
- I Never Stopped Liking You 115
- Time With You 116

8th Letter **117**
- Cuddling 119
- You Are Happiness 120
- Forever With You 121

9th Letter **122**
- Why I'm Single 124
- Wrong or Right 125
- Our Journey to Forever 126

10th Letter **127**
- We Reflect Each Other 129
- Love Out of Time 130
- You're My Conclusion 131

11th Letter **132**
- Vows to Love and to Care 133

About the Author **134**

Little things to look for...

Whispers (*.w. I love you*)

You will find *whispers* at the bottom of each page.

You know, that moment when you've expressed your heart to someone. And when you're done you give them a hug as you take a deep emotional breath and exhale sweet soft words into their ear.

Like the words *I love you so much* just to get one last word in.

That is what *Whispers* represents.

An Inspired Heart /A Broken Heart

You will find these at the top right hand corner of each page.

An *Inspired Heart* symbolizes a piece inspired by love.

A *Broken Heart* symbolizes a piece inspired by pain.

Words From my Heart by Amos Pinnock

...and with his heart on his sleeve,
    his heart decided to take control of his hand
        and wrote down all of his deepest thoughts...

1ˢᵗ Letter...

Dear Future Wife,

I promise from the moment I lay eyes on you my heart will sync with yours and share a beat. When you're excited, I'm excited, when you're sad I'm sad, when you're happy I'm happy. My heart will speed up and slow down with yours.

    Forgive me if I love you beyond understanding. Forgive me if I put your feelings before mine and make sure I'm on my grind every day so you can enjoy and cherish the time we spend together. I will treasure you as my one and only lover.

    Chasing forever and placing it into your hands, I'll build our future on God, Love, Faith and Goodness only heaven can provide. Yes! Heaven, because every moment spent with you, we leave time and enter eternity and it feels like heaven how you change even a stormy night into a summer's day.

    I have so much more to say, but you leave me speechless to the point where tears have to intervene and talk for me.

    From the bottom of my heart, I love you, I adore you and my heart will be a home for you to keep.

Yours Sincerely,
Amos. C. Pinnock

An Inspired Heart

The Start of Our Beginning

Your presence causes me to fear your absence.

Lonely at first sight, I wanted you in my life.

Thoughts of you rioted through my mind, breaking into the bank of my heart and loitering in the safe of my emotions. You left a beautiful mess that made the front page of my mind every morning. You became a terrorist, and I loved it. Blowing up my face with smiles, I couldn't help but sound an alarm that would-alert the Special Forces in my heart to take action and capture you.

I want you!

Two-second conversations became minutes. Thirty-minute conversations became an hour, Hours became days until days were never the same without hearing from you. Even though distance separated us, we became so close at heart that you were no longer a want but a need, and with you as a need the very thought of you being absent brings me to my knees, asking God to make you forever present in my life, and your absence forever absent.

As I see the fruits of my prayer blossom in you, I will water you with love to keep you alive in my life, because I can't see a life without you.

.w. I appreciate you...

An Inspired Heart

Love in the Moment

Sorry, but I don't know what's going to happen tomorrow or within the next five hours. All I care about is captivating and taking advantage of now, this moment, here, with you.

If I could see the future and know that tomorrow is definitely going to come, and that I'll have another day to spend happily with you, I'd be more held back and relaxed. But I don't, so every chance I get I want to inhale your presence and exhale love.

I'll give you random kisses and hugs because there's no other person in the world I'd rather share them with. I'll get to know more about you and give you my undivided attention. I'd make you laugh till your belly hurts and have you shed tears of joy. I'd give you gifts that will symbolise and be an ornament of my love.

Lost in each other's arms, we'll forget there's such thing as time. Captivated in each other's embrace, Love silences everything around us and the only thing we can hear are our heartbeats talking through Morse Code. I'll happily make plans for tomorrow as a Plan B, but my Plan A is to make the most of what we have right now and let the 3 words *I love you* unite 2 of us in 1 moment, and that moment is now.

I hope moments with you will last a lifetime.

.w. let's live for now...

An Inspired Heart

I Am Grateful

I have found *forever* within the numbered days we have on this Earth.

You found a love in me I never knew was there; you pulled it out and caused me to find peace within myself, the peace to know I am loved for me. I didn't have to change who I am, I didn't have to act like someone else. You accepted my flaws and problems, and somehow made them your own so I didn't have to feel alone while I was – am - going through them.

Your love helped me heal.

In all the places in the world, it's in your arms I truly felt safe, because I knew no matter what life threw at me you would stand by my side, supporting me all the way. Even when I was wrong, your actions of love corrected me, not holding anything against me, but moving forward we left mistakes in the past while pursuing happiness, and for that I know with no doubt in my being that I love you!

I adore and treasure your very existence in my life. I'm humbled, blessed and truly grateful that God created a love made just for me that is found in you.

And because I've found security in knowing out of 7 billion people, you are made just for me, you have my heart and I yours. You are my love, I love to love you for you, and for me.

.w. I will cherish you forever...

An Inspired Heart

At First Sight

Forgive me if I stare, but the moment I saw you, it was like the clouds opened up and a ray of sunlight shone down on you.

An angel, right before my eyes, speechless and overwhelmed with emotions, I tried to look away but I couldn't. I became blind to everything around me but you, deaf to all sounds but your voice and numb to every feeling except the feelings that have sprung up in my body for you. Goosebumps spread like a rash on my skin as I become conscious of my breathing, because each breath suddenly became heavy.

I've always thought stargazing happened at night, but today you've left me star struck.

You've destroyed my mind. Looking at you, I've seen the best that life can offer so I can never settle for less, and since you're the best, you've left my mind in a mess. I cannot focus properly. You're my beautiful distraction and until I have you permanently in my life, I will go on pursuing you as my mind replays the moment I first laid eyes on you. Deep down I feel I don't deserve you because you seem too good to be true, but that's more of a reason for me to cherish you if you ever become the ultimate special addition to my life.

.w. you captivate me...

An Inspired Heart

Goodbye to Goodbyes

Never do I want to say goodbye; never do I want to see you fade away into the distance never to return.

I don't want to see a sunset and sunrise without your head on a pillow next to mine. I don't ever want to feel like time's running out, making now our last moment. I don't want you to desert my island of love as you are the only population on it. I don't want to see you finding comfort in someone else's arms unless it's family.

I want my hand to be your gloves when it's cold. I want to see our love live on and stay strong with memories achieved in our hearts and minds as we get old.

I'm not obsessive, I just know deep down in my heart there's not a soul that can replace you, nor a day or year on the earth that would be worth living without you in it.

You've become so much a part of me that I feel like I won't be able to function properly if you ever left me. You're my second and better half. Like Eve to Adam, you're my missing link. You complete me.

So to keep your distance distant, I'll do all I can to forever keep you close to my heart, present in my life, because losing you will be like losing my breath.

.w. I can't be without you...

My
Little Love
Notes...

....

I don't want any more friends. I want the
helicopter of someone's love to land on my heart
and call my love paradise island...

....

Find someone that gives you no reason
to doubt and every reason to love...

A Broken Heart

Selfish

Wishing you all the happiness in the world isn't easy when I want to be one of the reasons you find it. I'm sorry if I sound selfish, but you have me feeling this way.

Every happy moment I experience somehow you're the person I want to have it with. I want to hold you and have my body heat warm you up, I want to spend endless time with you till it seems like we're in eternity. I want to be around when you complain, laugh, moan and talk just to hear your sweet voice.

I want to be the first one to say *happy birthday* to you, and spend that day with you in a special way.

Laughter massages the heart and if someone else is making you laugh they might get in. I don't like how someone else can make you laugh until tears run down your face. That's supposed to be me.

I want to be the person you fall asleep with and wake up to. My love for you is crazy, it's screaming out for you and only you, it refuses to open up for any other person but you. This is why I'm selfish. I want you and you only.

Sorry... but I'm not sorry.

A Broken Heart

Walls of Your Emotions

I'm done trying to entertain the walls of your emotions.

Titanium or brick, drilled or hammered, I can't seem to get through the walls of the maze your emotions bring. No signs, no signals, no hints, no clues, no way am I stressing over you, I refuse. I've got love to give, so why am I going around in circles trying to find the centre of your heart when all roads called "questions" with you lead to a dead end.

I don't know why I reassure you with words followed by actions, stamp comfort into your mind and heart when you don't apply the same method to me. It's never been vice versa with you, even now, as friends. The effort you deliver freezes my heart and the only thing that melts it is the heat of hope.

But I am optimistic. One day, the fiery love I have for you will burn your walls down, allowing you to see without the bricks of past hurts, pains, confusion and lack of trust blinding your eyes.

I'm not a virus. There's no need for you to put a firewall up against me. But……

With no signs, no signals, no hints and no clues, no way am I stressing over you. I refuse. You will no longer bruise my heart, but when your walls come down, hopefully I'll be around and my feelings won't [yet] have fallen apart.

A Broken Heart

Trust My Love

How can I love you if you keep pushing me away with your fears?

I'm not going to hurt you; my love will never result with you being in pain. My intentions towards you are to have you experience different scales of happiness, plus I want to show you that even you can experience a fearless love.

Don't walk away from me when I've done nothing wrong. If you do, yes, I will chase after you, because I know somewhere deep inside you want to be loved and your meek heart taken care of.

I won't bail out on you. I'm not after your flesh or sex. I'm after your heart. Let me in so I can help mend the broken pieces, break down the walls of fear and build a castle of happiness, love and trust so you, my Queen, can rule your heart with an untamed love like you've never been hurt before.

My desire is for us to have a love that's like an unquenchable fire, never to burn out, always bright and warming up your spirit.

Please, trust me to love you like you've never experienced pain and I promise you that from now until forever, our love will bring you nothing but happiness and joy.

A Broken Heart

Is it Just Me?

Hello! Is anyone there?

Is there anyone in this world who will love me how I'll love them? Why does it feel like I'm constantly paying for the damages of someone's past? I'm not them. I'm not going to put strings on your heart and play you like a puppet. The shoes your ex once walked in on the paths of your life are not my shoe size, so stop trying to find a reason to fit me into them.

I don't like the feeling of being emotionally drained. If I fill you up with love, you should do the same for me. I shouldn't be left empty while you're energised and overdosed on the confidence that I truly love you. I'm here trying to seek hints and signs that will help me see if you feel the same way. This isn't a game of I Spy, I tell you how it is, I don't leave you guessing and searching for answers, so shouldn't you do the same?

I shouldn't have to be the one who pops up every morning wishing you a good day for you to talk to me. Yes, it's nice to open your eyes to a beautiful message, but if you open your eyes before I do, I expect to see you put in the same effort that I do for you. I believe you know someone's intentions by their efforts. If someone really cares about something, they'll do all they can to sustain that thing in their life. This is how I feel. I hope I'm not alone with these thoughts.

So hello! Is anyone there?

My Little Love Notes...

··

He looked past her outwards appearance, saw her heart and thought, *she is the most beautiful thing that has walked through the corridors of my mind...*

··

Love brings sacrifice; sacrifice might bring pain but because you love, the pain is all worth it...

An Inspired Heart

In My Arms

Rest in my arms. Let me hold you till the night falls and day rises.

I want to take you into my heart and guide you down its hallway to the room I have prepared for you. I never want to let you go.

With my arms wrapped around your body and your head on my chest, listen to my heart and hear it telling you that I love beyond human understanding, that all that matters is me spending my lifetime with you and that my timeline is continuously marked with unforgettable moments spent with you.

As I kiss your head, I hope it sends a warm pulse to your mind letting it know that this is real, you won't have to worry about this being a one-time thing.

This is forever.

I will care for and protect you because you're the Queen of my Heart. My hands will never caress another person's hand the way it does to yours. Please believe, these are not only words of my love; they will be given life by the actions that follow them.

So as I hold you, let me show you my heart and welcome you into a world full of nothing but love and happiness.

An Inspired Heart

A Love for All to See

There's no hiding.

I couldn't care less about what people say or think about you, your past or even us. I will love you openly. I will show you off in public.

No, you're not a trophy, but if a man loves his car he'll show it off for everyone to see because he's proud of it. He knows it has value and it shows everyone the fruits of his labour and his accomplishments.

For me, you're my accomplishment, a statement and living proof that dreams and prayers do come true, that it's not only in Disney true love is found and one lives happily ever after. You're my happily ever after, my Princess. It's the night I kissed your lips under the light of a thousand stars where I found myself turned into a Prince.

You're the spark my heart needed to ignite its unquenchable fire of love, now ready to make you melt inside.

I can't keep quiet about you when my heart screams out how much I adore you more than life. You're my pride and joy, I have no reason to hide you, so let haters hate while we love.

This time love isn't blind. It's shining brightly for all to see. It's a sun that can never burn out.

.w. you're my pride and joy...

A Broken Heart

I Hate Our Distance

No, I'm not ok.

I don't want to *imagine* spending time with you anymore. I want to actually be with you and live the moments I imagine in my head. I miss you. I want you here with me.

I wish I could just kill the very distance that separates us, suck up the ocean that parts me from you, pull you right next to me and hold you with the intention of never letting you go.

I don't like being out alone on nights where the air is all warm and cosy for cuddling, while the sky is filled with stars ready to be wished on and the grass is as soft as a mattress ready to be laid upon.

I'm starting to despise every couple I see but at the same time wish they were you and me.

I don't like this distance. I want to be right in front of your face with my lips ready to press against yours. I hate this distance. It's cold and ugly.

I want you so badly.

Just to feel you locked in my arms, my chest pressed against yours and feeling our hearts hugging would be perfect.

Facing the reality of our distance hurts so bad, sometimes the only way to escape the pain is to fall asleep and hope I will meet you in my dreams. But even then, if I did, I wouldn't want to wake up.

Every day I think about the day I'll finally be with you, and when that day comes we'll make the most of the precious time we have together. I love you and this distance isn't going to change that, but my love for you doesn't stop the pain I feel.

I miss you as I sit here wishing there wasn't thousands of miles between us.

An Inspired Heart

Phone Calls

I'd fall asleep on the phone to you every night...

...just to wake up to your voice and share my first good mornings with you.

I wouldn't mind if we're on the phone and you're busy doing other things. There's something about just knowing you're there, hearing your voice and hearing you breathe, randomly calling your name just to have the warm tone of your voice send tingles down my spine.

I love how whenever we talk, I literally feel right next to you. I love hearing about your day, hearing you complain about the most random things, having deep conversations about life, starting fights over the phone that result in laughter, hearing you talk nonsense when you're tired and saying random things that come to mind. You always manage to print a smile on my face.

We're so unconscious of time, hours fly by without us even knowing.

I love the way you make long walks seem short and short walks long. You make good days hard because I can't stop thinking about calling you and sharing everything that has happened in my day. You make hard days easy when I know you're just a call away to happiness. Each time you call, I get excited like it's your first time calling; every time you speak, I fall deeper in love.

Don't ever stop calling, because even though you're not physically next to me, I feel as if you are.

.w. your voice is sweet music to my ears...

A Little
Random Thought

Lack of communication can bring lack of commitment. A person can find comfort in communicating with someone else in a way they should be communicating with you, and because you're absent in communication, they find themselves committing to someone who actually communicates with them...

A Broken Heart

Hate That I Love You

OMG, as if you're still raiding my belly with butterflies!

We hardly talk but that doesn't stop you from being number one in my heart. I know without a doubt I'll be here for you even if you don't want me to. Yes, we're no longer together, but my heart will still provide wings of love for you to fly with. I've still got your back till the very end.

I love you more than you'll ever know.

It's weird because when you find someone else, yes, I'll be jealous, but I'll be here for you. I'll be celebrating with you when he fills your heart with joy, but if he ever hurts you, I'll be a shoulder you can lean on, helping you through your problems.

Your happiness is precious to me and I'll do all I can to ensure life brings you vast amounts of it. I have no clue on how you feel towards me, but regardless of that, please know I love you, care for you and I'm here for you.

You'll always have your own room in my heart.

.w. I'll always be here when you need me...

A Broken Heart

Show Me Your Love

I hate the fact that others show me the love and attention I crave from you.

    Yes I'm comparing, because I don't like that someone else is giving me the effort I want from you. I'll make sure I give you 100% of me, so no one can show or make you feel something that you aren't already feeling. I don't ever want you to experience lack of love, so you'll have no reason to go and find it in someone else.

    I make sure I look presentable and on point so your head won't have to turn when you're out with me. I make sure I do all I can to please you and make you happy, I make sure I give you my phone off, ears open undivided attention, so that I won't miss a single a moment with you.

    Call me selfish, but you're mine and I don't want anyone else to have you, because when I said you're my one and only I meant it. So I'll do anything I can to keep you as the only one.

    But, what I can't seem to understand is why you don't act the same way towards me. I'm not asking for a lot when I say put some effort in and actions to your words. Even though others are showing me the effort and love I want from you, I will never leave what we have and move on to them.

    Why? Because I want to share all that love has to offer with you and only you.

    Forgive me if I offended you, but their attention doesn't go unnoticed. All I'm asking is that you make the attention of others become unnoticeable.

    Make *your* love and effort noticeable.

A Broken Heart

Just a Memory

I'm afraid to close my eyes because, they only open to memories of you...

...memories so vivid and strong they carry a weight of emotions experienced in the time we spent together.

I can't escape these thoughts. It seems so impossible to evacuate these feelings that still linger in the alleys of my heart. And even though memories of you have been evicted out of my heart leaving them homeless, I can't help but throw pity change of emotions at the feet of what we had.

I admit when I see you I do think *'What if we had given love a try? Would all the fighting have stopped? Would you have finally opened up and told me how you felt? Could we have stamped years onto our relationship progress card?'*

But I will never pose those questions to you. The last thing I want to do is lead you on making you feel there's a ray of hope shining through the grey clouds of our friendship, making you hope for a future of you and me becoming one.

Our equation came out odd not even, so we were never on the same emotional level and I couldn't handle that.

What we had will stay as a memory, because only a fool makes the same mistakes and expects different results.

I will not make the same mistake again.

My Little Love Notes...

He loved her so much that even the *thought* of hurting her brought him pain. So he did all he could just to make sure she remained happy...

When he finds getting to know you as a person more exciting than getting to know your body, then you know he's really for you...

2nd Letter...

Dear Future Wife,

I had a dream about you last night and I can't wait for the days I can wake up and see your face and thank God I'm living the dream.

Reality no longer exists because God obviously gave me what I thought was impossible to get. YOU!

You're the star I gaze upon day and night. You never fail to shine because your beauty is so divine and unique, I get butterflies every time you speak. YOU!

You inspire me, motivate me, your smile is your best curve, you're a gift to life I feel like I don't deserve because YOU!

Your imperfections make you perfect. Through every storm and hard time, the fight I'd give! I know you're worth it because YOU!

You were only found by the star that once led 3 wise men to a baby in a manger. That Star led me to my Queen, my future, the love of my life. YOU!

So whoever you are, out of the 7.125 billion people in the world, I hope you find this message, so we can wake up and dream together.

Yours Sincerely,
Amos. C. Pinnock

An Inspired Heart

I Want to Strip Your Heart

You don't need to strip for me to love you.

    I fell in love with you before I noticed your body. Your smile was the first thing I noticed; I instantly thought, *Wow, if I could just see that smile every day, there will be no need for a sun in the sky because that smile lights up my world.*

    Yes you have an amazing figure, and if I had powers to alter it I wouldn't change a thing, but that's not what caught my attention. If one day you lost an arm or a leg, I'll still love you the same way. If you ended up in a wheelchair, I'd roll you down the aisle and still declare you as my wife *to love and to cherish, to have and to hold, through sickness and through health, till death do us part.*

    My love for you is a bond beyond what human eyes can see. It's internal.

    I'm more interested in stripping your heart and loving the beauty inside it rather than stripping your body and being inside you. What I feel for you is not lust but love and I will always love you from the inside out. Why?

    Because your heart was the first thing I fell in love with.

An Inspired Heart

Investment of Love

When you said you loved me for the first time...

...my body became so weak I thought I was going to fall. I started breathing so hard my heart started to race; you turned my life upside down. New plans for the future were shown to the boardroom of my mind, a project called 'The One". It involved involving you in all the happiness I experience.

You're one of the greatest investments I've had for developing my very being, I want to better myself, work harder and push beyond limits, and not just for me but for us. I want to do all I can to ensure the insurance of my love doesn't just give you a quote of how I will love you, but that my actions will follow up, making sure you have no need and reason to claim someone else's love.

I'll try my best to make sure you never go without, even if it means I'll sacrifice my very best to give you the best; I will do it. Because there's not a day on this Earth where I don't want you to feel wrapped in the duvet of love, warming you up in every season of life we go through. We may hit some hard bumps along the way, but they will never break the suspension of love we have for one another. Loving you is the best job in the world. I will never resign nor quit, because I know each time I invest love in you...

...life will only get better.

.w. I will never stop loving you...

An Inspired Heart

I Feel Your Pain

I don't ever want you to go through any pain on your own.

    With God as my witness, if I could take on your pain to see a smile resurrect on your face, I would. There won't be a night or day that'll go by where I won't pray that God takes into His hands any affliction you face and brings comfort to your mind body and soul.

    I swore from the moment I met you I'll care for your needs and tend to your emotions as if they we're my own. I will stand by you regardless of the outcome, for better for worse, through sickness and in health; death will have to be the only alternative to part us, but even then you'll live on in my heart.

    Don't ever think you'll be a burden on me. I count every single breath you take as a blessing and I'm more than willing to give up my own life for yours. Yes, that sounds crazy but my love is crazy when it comes to you, and I'll destroy the phrase 'the skies the limit' because my love for you is limitless.

    So whatever comes your way, please know and understand, I am here for you no matter what.

    Your life, happiness and the love we share is what matters to me.

.w. no matter what, I will stand by you...

I Can't Help But Miss You

My arms have never felt so empty.

I hope the memories we created will be a medicine to take away the pain of loneliness when you're not around.

Closing my eyes is so hard when your head is not next to mine. Regardless if you're gone for a nine to five day at work, a month or a year, I still miss you, but the feeling can be a beautiful pain. It makes me more excited to see you and I can't wait for the sound of your voice to make love to my ears.

Just knowing you're out of my personal space makes me want no space between us. You bring a smile to my face that no one else can; you don't have to do much, it's just you.

I realise how precious time is when it's spent with you, because I know we both know time waits for no man, so the fact that it seems like it slows down just for us to have more time together is special; it makes us value what we have together.

The beauty of knowing our goodbyes have an expiry date lights up my world. Our goodbyes are not the end but the beginning of missing you. That might sound weird but missing you makes me appreciate your presence even more, and a rich bottle of emotions is prepared, shaken up and ready to be poured out on you when we're together again.

It's noted in my heart we're together forever, but that doesn't stop me from missing you when you're not around.

I need you like the day needs the sun and the night, the moon.

My Little Love Notes...

I hope one day the effort and love I put in will come back to me. I'm tired of always giving so much and never receiving...

Sometimes you have to create your own smile, find your own joy and seek after your own happiness...

A Broken Heart

We Had To Stop Talking

I'm sorry we had to stop talking.

It's just knowing I couldn't have you was killing me on the inside. You said you had feelings for me but were still trying to figure out life, while I wanted you to become a part of my life. I still have feelings for you, I can say they'll always be here but that'll be a lie.

It annoyed me that other girls came along, showed me the attention, affection and feelings I wanted from you.

I mentally tagged your name on every love song I heard. I imagined ways to shower you with happiness and love when we'd finally met. Now, all of that has to be pushed away.

I don't know what will happen between us.

Shall I move on?

See, that's even hard because I'll always think, *what if we gave love a try, instead of finding every excuse to avoid it because of fear?* I don't know if I'll ever know, but just so you know, every time I see your picture, a smile climbs on my face as my mind says, *she is so beautiful.*

I won't be stubborn but understanding, so I hope you find what you want in life and it brings you all the happiness you deserve.

As for me and you, well, I don't know what life will bring. I will try to wait for you. I'm not saying it will be easy, but somewhere in my heart...

...I hope you will be worth the wait.

A Broken Heart

Her Apology for My Pain

I don't want to live without your smile making my day.

    I made a mistake, I understand, I didn't realise how much you filled that empty, emotionless void in my heart. You had me feeling a love I wasn't used to. Because of past pains I found it weird and I thought you were playing a game, so I pushed you away.

    And each time you came back my actions made it seem like I just kept pushing and pushing and pushing you away, but honestly I didn't mean to. I just didn't know how to act.

    I wish I could have you back.

    I'm sorry.

    I should have told you how I felt towards you. I should have told you how you made me feel alive. You gave me a new smile each day I woke up to your heart-felt messages. I shouldn't have made you pay for his mistakes. I should have taken the muzzle off my emotions and made them speak out to you, at least then you wouldn't have felt like your feelings were going one way.

    I hate living the quote, "you never really know what you've got till it's gone". I just hope your feelings haven't fully gone. I don't know if you ever want to hear from me again, but if I could say something to you, I'd say *I'm sorry*.

    And if the stars could ever make my wishes come true, I'll have you back...

    ...and love you like you've never been loved before.

A Broken Heart

Never Going Back

I'm moving on.

I'm going to leave what we had in the past instead of having it linger in my present. I'm no longer giving life support to a dead thing, so I'm pulling the plug. Because the energy I'm wasting on you could go to someone that makes me feel alive, welcomed and happy. I'm done reserving a room for you in my heart, thinking one day you're going to come in and make it home.

You had your chance and now it's gone, so when my distance becomes present to you, don't draw close, don't express any type of emotions; my ears are closed. I no longer sympathise with you nor pay any attention, because when I tried to show you attention, you never gave me the time of day, so my day has no spare or reserved time for you.

Please don't come with any explanations about why you had acted a certain way, because I will happily send you and your explanation away.

The old me would welcome you with open arms just to see you happy, but now I've found happiness for myself. I see my true value. I don't need to settle for less than I deserve. I'm not saying you don't deserve to be loved, I'm just saying the love I have is not for you.

So as I move forward and put you behind me, I wish myself the best, and that all the love, effort and happiness I give out will be given back to me.

A Little
Random Thought

Have you been in that moment where you just want to feel loved, to feel like you matter to someone and to know that they care about you so much they'll put in as much effort as you put into them, giving you no reason to be afraid of getting hurt or getting your heart broken?

Oh Girl

Oh girl, will you promise you'll be mine? Till the end of time?

All I want is that security that my heart will be your diamond centrepiece, to complete you totally, making me feel complete, like you're my destiny.

Oh girl, I cannot define how important it is for me to love you. I feel like my heart is glued to you and no matter what I do, I can't escape from you.

So with this knowledge, I promise that you will get all of me, my love will aim to please you, will make you happy and will keep you warm inside.

Oh girl, wishes are made each night, just to keep you forever next to me. I don't want to see a night or day rise where your eyes aren't the first and last pair of eyes I see, because in your eyes, I see a future, I see my home, I see a love that grows.

So every day, I promise to remind you that I love you and that there's no one in this world that can replace you.

Oh girl, you give me reason to live, and I'm happy to live a life of loving you.

An Inspired Heart

Let Me Fall in Love with You

Please can I see you... the girl behind the foundation, extensions and eyeliner?

I want to know... the girl behind the hundreds of Instagram Likes and Twitter Re-Tweets.

I want to see you... the unique and wonderfully made creation from God, the girl no one knows or sees behind closed doors, the person you set free when eyes aren't present.

Let me fall in love with her.

I want to love your insecurities and kiss the scars you're afraid to show; I want to see your fears and help you become brave; I want to hold the hand that got pushed away and have you find peace in knowing I'm here to stay; I want to fall in love with the girl that's slow at times and finds the weirdest things funny, with the girl that cries at everything and wants that extra attention when it's her time of month.

I'm here to understand, get to know and listen to everything that comes out of your beautiful mouth.

You is what I want. You don't have to act or try to be anything for me to accept you in my heart, It's the raw you I'm dying to fall crazy in love with. Because I know there's no other you in the world.

And I want you...

...to become my world.

.w. don't be afraid to be yourself...

An Inspired Heart

I Won't Wait Till You're Gone to Love You

I'm not going to wait till you're gone to appreciate you.

I'm not waiting till you reach your last breaths to tell you that I love you. I don't want to live on old memories because we can't create new ones, so while you're here, present, with me, I will make the most of you being in my life. Even if it means you get annoyed with me telling you how much you mean to me, I don't care. I will bombard you with all the compliments, kind and loving words I can say, because I really don't have a clue in this world when your or my time is up. So while I'm here with you we'll make every second count, never numbering days but adding memories to the collection box we hold close and dear in our hearts.

If I could, I'd take your hand and run away with you from time so we could have forever with each other. We won't have to worry about tomorrow because days will never end.

But since that can't happen, each day we live, I will love and care for you, be there for you and keep you close to my heart.

Because I'm not going to wait till you're gone to appreciate you. I'm not going to wait for your last heartbeat to show you I love you.

.w. I'll make every moment count...

My Little Love Notes...

I can't wait to stare into the eyes of the one I love and see the thousands of stars I wished upon to get her...

Her happiness is worth more than diamonds; that's why I feel like the richest man alive whenever she smiles...

An Inspired Heart

The Beautiful Switch

Time, please just stay still.

Let me live this moment till I feel I am satisfied with how my heart reacts to this angel standing in front of me.

A world full of billions of people but all I can see is you. I refuse to turn my head or look away, because that could mess up the connection our hearts have made through our eyes.

There are no musicians around but I can hear soft violins playing in the background, a melody that sets the scene for you and I to make the next move.

Dare I take this moment lightly?

Let me take your hand and pull you in closer to me. I want to hear you exhale as I whisper into your ear, *this is our moment, our time, right here, right now.*

Let's take control and get lost in each other's presence. I won't let you go till you tell me to. As my arms are wrapped around your body and yours around mine and as our eyes slowly close and lips touch, we stamp our mark on each other, symbolising the bond and unity we now share.

My lips will only touch your lips now and forever; my heart will only sync with yours and this bond we have created will never be broken because of this moment...

...this moment where our hearts climbed through the windows of our eyes and switched bodies.

Shy Around You

I'm a confident guy, but around you I get shy.

I will be the man for you, but you bring the child out of me. When I see your face, I get all excited like a kid in a sweet shop. I get all lost for words till I start talking nonsense, but even then you play along and we have the most amazing conversations about the most random things.

There's no need to act like a character around you, you allow me to be me. You tore up the manual script people tried to place on our relationship, enabling us to freestyle and create our own way of living while loving.

Boredom got bored of trying to be our friend; it never found its place in our circle. The sun got jealous because you would be the one who would always brighten up my day. I'm happy we can rule each other's hearts with a love that's death to people's opinions and negative thoughts, also caring not to care too much about problems but, making sure they never accrue again.

And even though you make my knees go weak, my love will stand up strong for you.

There will be times where I'll act childish just to make you care about me that little bit more, but know I will always be your soldier, your bodyguard and your man.

.w. your love makes me feel like jelly...

My Little Love Notes...

....

I crave a fearless love. Loving with faith and not sight, we'll walk to our freedom. Free to love unconditionally like we've never been hurt...

....

Baby, my love stands strong for you, my knees bow in faith and my heart offers up prayers for us...

3rd Letter...

Dear Future Wife,

I just woke up and found myself praying, well, praying for you.

    I was asking God to guide and protect you in all aspects of life, to fulfil your heart's desires and bring you eternal happiness. That joy becomes your boat, peace, your ocean and love; the sunlight that shines all the days of your life. And if darkness was to come, hope will be a star that guides you like a lighthouse to the shores of comfort and rest.

    I prayed that God would help me help you. Help you with every need, help me understand and relate to you, care and tend to your emotions, and help me see from your point of view and perspective, instead of going on what I think I know.

    Then for us, that our love will be a bond so strong, if anything tries to break it, that thing will be broken. That if we fight, we fight for what's right and for each other. When we cry, they'll be tears of joy and happiness, and that in every moment spent together we'll get lost in our own world where nothing else exists except you and me.

    I believe I'm a prayer away from meeting you.

    Plus God knows the desires of the heart and you're a prayer my heart desires to come true.

    So I pray that somehow, this message will get to you.

Yours Sincerely,
Amos. C. Pinnock

An Inspired Heart

Always and Forever

Always and forever!

My heart found life when the words *I love you* left your mouth. I began to sink in a pool of love created by the tears of joy I found myself crying. No longer living a life of contentment, I finally felt complete, complete in knowing that I have gained an extra life to live, and that life is with you. Out of reality and into a dream I flew, as your love levitated me off my feet.

As soft as pillows your embrace became.

Bright like the sun our future looked.

Not taking notice of time, we lived each day like there was no beginning or ending.

God became our guide to a healthy and successful relationship. He had us find joy in situations that tried to drag us down. He made us value, cherish and abandon actions that contained pride and ignorance. We stuck to promises and stayed away from lies. We became a team, a partnership. We united our hearts, minds and souls, enabling us to be soul mates. We kept and are keeping true to each other in everything we do.

This is why I see always and forever in your eyes...

... and believe I'll have always and forever with you.

An Inspired Heart

Young Hearts

Young hearts sharing a love that never ages.

When I met you, I never knew the stars I once stared at in the sky were the same ones in your eyes. You moved me to a place of happiness I never thought I could reach, let alone physically see! You have become my happiness, my smile, and the owner of the butterflies - that storm in my belly each time your name is mentioned.

Joy is found in my heart when I hear you laugh; the glow around your body, your soft hands, your sweet voice and your dreamy eyes send me to heaven and back.

Every guy has a missing rib and you are mine.

Destiny is like a jigsaw puzzle. You're one of the pieces in mine and I'm glad life has given us enough time to explore the beauty of our destiny.

When we grow old together, our love will not have aged, but will still be young and free. We are young hearts, sharing an everlasting love.

I hope this love we share will keep you forever with me.

.w. at heart, we'll forever be young lovers...

A Little
Random Thought

Give your partner a reason to be loyal. If you're constantly absent, terrible at replying/talking and don't put that much effort and time into building your relationship, life has a way of presenting your partner with someone who does all of that in your absence, and sooner or later, you'll lose them to that person who was doing your job…

A Broken Heart

A Truthful Lie

"As long as you're happy."

Five words that represent five figures and a palm that slapped me in the face and made me realise that the deep meaning of those insane five words is, *I'll sacrifice my happiness for yours.*

You told me to hold back my feelings till the right time. You said you were not ready for you and-me to become us, plus you can't say how you feel because the fear past relationships has on you stops you from being able to peel the shell of your heart and share the fruits of love with me.

So I've got to wait.

And not knowing the time frame or length of this wait leaves me in a dark void of not knowing whether the wait will be worth it.

I don't understand how you expect me to hold back my feelings for you. That's like trying to put a lid on a volcano that's about to erupt. Knowing I have to bite my tongue and shut myself up when I want to express my feelings to you, makes no sense to me. It's like telling my heart to stop beating but I've got to stay alive.

It's not like I see you as just a friend, so it's not easy trying to act like one, but to make you feel comfortable, I agree with the decision you've made even though it hurts me deep inside. I'll sacrifice my happiness for yours.

You will never know or see the hurt, pain or sadness I feel, because I will happily lie to you through a smile or a laugh so you get the happiness you deserve.

And so those painful five words, *as long as you're happy*, leave my mouth.

A Broken Heart

A Life Sentence

I want to put my heart on death row.

I'm always, like, always coming out first, always saying how I feel and never really hearing anything back, leaving me with questions not answers, and unanswered questions are like 1000 blades to the heart.

Once again, regardless of past situations that reflect this one where I have opened up and got nothing but the sound of breathing, this time round it hurts!

It's not easy to always say how you feel and be the first to come out with it, too. It's not good how it's become normal for me to expect silence after my emotions literally screamed out to you.

So my heart will serve a life sentence, locked away from its suicidal acts of exploding with emotions (only words causing an explosion more powerful than an atomic bomb), intended to bring me happiness, love and care simultaneously.

This will be the only hope my heart has for freedom.

Then and only then, will I love again, with all the love within me.

My
Little Love
Notes...

Don't put me in the shoes your exes once walked in. My shoes won't walk all over you...

He always reminded himself how empty life would be without her, so he would never take advantage of how great life is with her...

Loneliness is Lonely

Before I was alone but now I'm not.

You being here with me has caused loneliness to leave my side forever. My sofa has never felt more comfortable since you've been on it; there's an extra place to lay my head and an extra pair of arms to hold me.

I look forward to spending time with you.

It's a whole new world to me. It's hard to explain but when we're together, reality shuts down and I'm in a fantasy world. The stars feel closer, the moon becomes our sofa, the sky is our blanket and dreams become reality.

My mind is at peace.

People spend their lives trying to find the executioner of loneliness, and when you stepped into my life, I knew I had found mine.

The rivers of my love will never cease from flowing into the ocean of your heart now; my heart and mind are at peace knowing that you are the reason; loneliness is no longer my partner and I promise I will make sure loneliness will never become yours.

An Inspired Heart

You Can Tell Me Anything

I couldn't care less about any wrong doings in your past.

Your imperfections will not push me away. Any issues or problems won't stop me from saying *I'm here to stay*, I will love you the same way.

Each day we live we'll aim to create a hopeful future and decorate our present with love, so when our present becomes our past, our past will be a beautiful thing to look at.

I won't judge or look down on you when any truth you're ashamed or afraid to tell is brought to my notice and attention. No one is perfect. Regardless of anything, my arms will be open for you to find comfort and peace in. I am here for you till the very end and all I ask of you is to be honest with me, even if it hurts.

I am willing to work out any situation that's tries to hinder you or us from moving forward in life and doing better and greater things. You can trust me, please believe nothing will be hidden from you. You will have a blueprint of my past problems, worries and troubles. There is nothing more precious than being able to vent to the person you love.

Unconditional love is the ability to love and be loved completely, regardless of what's happened or is happening.

I trust you. I just hope the love I show you allows you trust me too.

.w. this is a promise from me to you...

A Little
Random Thought

Having feelings one-way hurts and being emotionally drained kills. You don't need that stress. Your happiness is what matters, you have an amazing heart and if someone doesn't notice and cherish-it like it's their own beating heart, then they don't deserve you...

An Inspired Heart

You Make Me Happy

I love the way you have me wearing a smile like it's my daily uniform.

You flood my mind with happy thoughts that soon become a reality when we're face to face. I wish we could control the sky; I would turn it deep purple and have blue stars glitter its face, and there would be a soft warm breeze that would feel like a blanket covering us every time it blew.

But, even though these thoughts stay as a thing we imagine, I don't need all of that for a perfect night. You simply being next to me and wrapped up in my arms as our hearts connect and our minds clear of any problems is perfect enough for me. All that we're focused on is us, enjoying each and every kiss, taking random selfies to remember each moment and making the most of the time we've managed to share together.

You've become my daily dose of happiness and I never want this prescription to end.

Random Thought

If only you knew how much being with you means to me!

Just to feel your lips against my skin, my fingers in between yours and hearing your voice harmonise with mine as we say, "I love you." I just want to take you by the hand, pull you in close to me and never let you go. The magic I feel whenever I'm with you causes my heart to fly with the clouds.

Heartbeats race, as smiles invade the face because your lips left a beautiful taste on mine.

Here with you, I lose myself in deep emotions. Speechless I become because the deeper I get in falling in love with you, the more difficult it becomes for my mind to simulate words to describe the acres of love I have for you.

Oh! you beautiful human, let my love be a fire that you're happy to camp around.

Take my words as evidence and remember them, for my actions will follow up showing you that what I say is not a lie but the truth. I will love you with a love that makes fairy tales jealous. Happily ever after will be the closing statement to the story of our life.

I'm not ashamed to announce my love towards you to anyone and everyone. Let the galaxy hear me when I say I love you, let the stars write your name and mine in the sky for all to see.

I'm proud but humbled to be the lover of your heart, and more humbled that you are the lover of mine.

My
Little Love
Notes...

....

I believe a relationship is a partnership, meaning I will stand by you and support you no matter what...

....

There's only so much I can do to prove my love to you If you don't step out of fear and allow me to love you, then we can't move forward in our relationship...

Black Heart

You made me feel like we were something.

Like I was Romeo and you Juliet. You told me you loved me, you insinuated plans of a future together, made me feel like you were the only one for me out of billions of people. And when I was at the point of no return, leaving a single life to pursue a partnership with you, you left! Told me you're not looking for anything serious, you're pursuing a career when you weren't employed and appreciated me as a friend. Basically giving me the sugar coated version of "I'm not interested in you."

I don't understand how someone would give someone wings, and as they're about to take flight, cut them off.

Confused at the loss of life I thought I had in you, my heart has turned black and numb to all emotions. Because before you, I refused to open up, but hoping for a difference I thought I saw in you, I let you in, so I opened up trusting you with the valuable items of love in my heart.

At first it seemed like you valued them as much as I did making me trust you even more, but I guess I was wrong, because you single-handedly destroyed everything inside, making me close up, not just to you but to everyone. Making me put up walls I swore I'd never put up.

I don't need another friend I've got enough, so this is goodbye and I wish you all the best.

A Broken Heart

Just a Reminder

I'm confused.

Where did I go wrong? Is it wrong for me to love you so much and so hard? Could my love have been pressure on you?

I would say I could love less for a bit, but is that even legal in the laws of love?

I mean, love is patient, so I tried my best to wait for you while you mentally pushed a wall in front of me every time I tried to show you love.

Love is kind and I was nothing but kind to you, smiling even though you hurt me just to make you not feel bad for what you've done, being calm through every unnecessary mood swing you had, even though I had all the right to throw the biggest tantrum over all you don't do.

Love puts others needs before its own and that's all I did for you. Even if it meant I lacked, I still put your needs before mine.

So with all that's been seen and said, where could I have possibly gone wrong? To be honest, deep down in me I would like an answer, but I don't think I could handle staying calm once you've said it. There couldn't be a good answer that could make me understand why we went our separate ways, but if you weren't ready, why would you string me along making me feel like we shared a life, then leave me for dead and emotionally drained?

I'm not saying this to gain your sympathy or to hear you apologise, I just thought I'd make you aware of all I've done for you. And when you realise the value of the love I once had for you, please know it's gone and you can never get it back. But also when someone else shows you this amount of love, don't do the same to them as you did to me. They might not be as calm towards your simpleton mind-set of how to appreciate and value love.

A Broken Heart

I Wish We Could Have Been

I wish you could have stayed.

I can't believe I let you get away. You once walked upon the clouds of my dreams, but now, you're nowhere to be seen except in my memories. Your face appears and vanishes like breath on a cold day, your voice plays over in my head and your scent still lingers on my clothes.

I miss you.

I miss phones calls where we never even spoke. Just knowing you were there was a way I enjoyed your presence, and your presence made me feel loved. Oh how, if I could, I would turn back the hands of time and replay the moments where you and I started and finished a laugh together, where we would pray for one another in hope that it would keep us together. But once the prayers stopped our souls lost contact and our heart started beating different beats.

Now my lips sink and tears fall whenever I see a couple and think *this could have been us; if only we had given love a try we would still be together.*

I wish I didn't wait till you were gone to really see how much value you added to my life, how much I really love you and what you really mean to me.

If somehow we get a second chance at us, I'll give you my all without a second thought. But for now, I'll start praying for you again, praying you receive all the happiness and love in the world, because you deserve it.

But I'll regret it's not me giving it to you.

A Little
Random Thought

Love makes you stick around even when it hurts to. All the pain you experience, you're willing to go through. Hoping you'll prove that your love is more than true and to show that person they mean more than the world to you…

4th Letter...

Dear Future Wife,

Imma keep it 100, I believe in us.
 I believe that you and I will brave every storm and dark place life throws at us. I will stand by your side, even if it means I lose my life. Sounds extreme, but I am extremely in love with you and I will go to the extreme to see you extremely happy.
 Killing every negative vibe with a positive action, we'll cure the cancer of confusion, pain and hate. Understanding that we may misunderstand each other, but never allowing what's misunderstood, to a line, where and how we move forward.
 Our heads won't rest on a pillow until our minds and hearts are at rest with each other. I believe in us, and there's no doubt in my mind, as we kneel before God, we will stand before giants, hand in hand, heart to heart. And with my hand on my heart, I believe in us! As I believe one day, you'll receive this message.

Yours Sincerely,
Amos. C. Pinnock

An Inspired Heart

My Destiny

To you, my heart, my love, my all.

With our vows and promises bonded, sealed and placed onto our fingers, we become one in the sight of God. Two hearts united and forever true to the three words *I love you*. Hand in hand we step into a new life knowing nothing can separate what God has put together, me and you, you and me.

We will go through rough times, but even a diamond will go through a rough time to become a masterpiece, and so will we. We are the Master's piece of art, once separated by distance but now brought together by destiny.

Vowing never to hold back love but injecting it into each other's hearts, we recognise there's no such thing as an overdose.

So stepping out in love and faith as God our father walks with us in this journey we're taking, we ask him to guide and protect us through every happy and hard time; to educate and direct us so we can protect each other's hearts, and shape and mould us into the couple he wants us to be, not what others make us out to be.

With all I have and all my heart, I will love and be with you my friend, best friend and soul mate, till the end of time.

An Inspired Heart

A True Imagination

Today my eyes watered with joy because of you...

...and being overwhelmed with emotions, three teardrops said three words. *I love you*. But I feel like the words *I love you* are an understatement of how passionate I am towards you. Overdosed on the happiness you prescribed, it's not hard to wait and be patient for you, because I love the treatment and care you give and show to me. Freely I'll love you like every day is our last because I know what we have will last, and I enjoy the thought and fact that you'll be the first and last person I wake up and fall asleep to for the rest of my life.

Every time you blink I see a sunset and sunrise. Every time you smile your face lights up like stars in the night sky. I am with no doubt the luckiest guy in the world to have you, the definition of beauty, in my life.

My one and only, the only one, you will forever be the one for me.

.w. no one can ever take your place in my heart...

An Inspired Heart

Walking Without Friendship

The problem is I love her too much.

Countless hours of spending time with this imaginary girl in my night and day dreams, I found myself falling in love with her. But the question of who she is tortured me while I was awake because I gained a dangerous desire to sleep, for sleep was the only place we could meet. But one day, as I blinked, I saw her.

Wondering if I was asleep, I repeatedly blinked. Disney would call it love at first sight, but I've been in love with her since I've been able to dream.

Approaching her in amazement, she had me at *hello*. We automatically clicked and it felt like we've known each other in a previous life only to be joined once again.

Finding ourselves in each other, we thought we found love. Agreeing to walk and take things slow, I realised we were lying because our hearts were racing, and with our hearts racing with emotions and our minds going slow and not really getting to know each other, we didn't know where we stood.

We didn't have a foundation of friendship, causing us to fall and realise we're still strangers.

Now taking it slow seemed like a problem because my heart became inpatient, and craved its daily dose of love. I started hating the presence of her friendship and hating the absence of her love, but I knew if we gave our hearts what they wanted, we would find ourselves falling and not have a friendship to fall upon when times got hard.

So neutralising my heart, I started to dream and imagine us being friends, hoping one day my heart will wake with a foundation of friendship to stand on enabling us to love once again.

An Inspired Heart

Love

Loving only hurts when you love the wrong person.

It's like wearing the wrong size shoes; no matter how much you try to squeeze into them, they'll be too small and tight for you. It's the same with love. Not just anyone and everyone can handle your capacity of love.

Love brings a great deal of sacrifice and sacrifice can sometimes bring pain. Now, you know the sacrifice is out of love when one see's the beauty of the pain and understands the pain will bring a profitable gain.

It's like a woman with child. Because she loves the child inside of her she will go through nine months of sacrificing her figure, image and way of life, doing all she can to protect her child. Plus during labour she's willing to go through pain knowing she'll gain a beautiful child out of it. That's true love!

For God so loved the world that He gave His only son to die so we can have life.

Sacrifice shows love, love shows sacrifice.

Now, love is patient. If they're not patient they don't love you. If someone really loves you, their love will be an anchor that holds them down in the ocean of your heart. But in order for someone to wait and be patient they have to have repetitive reassurance that the wait is not in vain. Reassurance will sustain the life of their love for you and help them enjoy the wait.

The most important thing is never to hold back on love, love was never made to be tamed but to run wild and free. Taming love is like tying the wings of an eagle and telling it to fly. You've bound its potential and purpose. So let your love roam free and if someone is trying to tie the wings of your love down, they do not deserve your love.

Protection

I will protect you.

    May God forgive me if I do something crazy to ensure that I keep to that promise. I refuse to let any harm or danger present itself to you. You are my world, so I won't let negative pollution of people's words or actions corrupt or poison my mind to make me think differently about you.

    I pray The Lord will stand and hear the prayers I send up to Him to protect and guide you, for with His guidance you can't go wrong and with His protection you'll face no harm.

    Since you're a part of me, I care dearly about you and the way you feel.

    It's no lie when I say I will do whatever I can within my power to make you happy. Standing by you will not be a problem because I made a vow that is imprinted in my heart to support you no matter what. Come hell or high water I will be there. I don't care if my knees get scars from always kneeling in prayer, the God of angel armies is always by our side and I know, as I seek Him, He will listen and answer.

    God knows the desires of the heart, and one of mine is that He is your personal body guard wherever you go and in whatever you do. I am not afraid because I know He has got you, and I'm happy He's protecting you because He is basically protecting my heart.

.w. I've got your back to the very end...

Cry

Cry on my shoulder, let it all out.

I don't care if my t-shirts get soaked with your tears, I'm here, here with an ear that will listen to your every moan and groan. Tell me what's up, what's causing your heart pain and sorrow. Don't stop till all you've held in has been let out, giving your heart room for comfort, happiness and joy. Don't be afraid to go all out and say how you truly feel, I won't judge you. I might not even understand, but what I want you to understand is that I'm here for you. Don't shut up what needs to be let out. Sadness can be a beautiful thing because it allows one to bring, plus give you the comfort and love needed for you in that moment and time.

So let them tears fall and run down your face, allow your eyes to go red as snot runs down your nose and heavy breaths take over. Let go and free your emotions, because they will end up setting you free by clearing your mind of all the things you've bottled up.

Take as long as you like, I'll be right here, with you, by your side, ready to comfort, support and love you through it all.

My
Little Love
Notes...

....

You were once a stranger, I didn't even know you existed, but now, you're someone I can't live without, and the closest thing to my heart...

....

They started off as friends, became lovers and ended up as Husband and Wife...

To You

I love you so much; you don't know what you've done to me.

You've literally became the heart of my heart. Everything I wanted and needed to hear, you have said. Your words have been the password that has unlocked the safe of my love, making it open up to you. "The One's" identity has been found, my future has been seen and my everything is you. Each time I look at you, I fall in love, smiles rush to my face and my heart starts to race each time you inject love into me. I'm happy because I know you'll never stop.

I trust you.

I know for a fact you won't hurt me or stop transferring magnanimous amounts of love into the life savings account in my heart making me rich in love. You're too good to be true. I can't help but think I'm dreaming; never in a million years did I think I would be with someone as beautiful and loving as you.

I just never thought it would be you. You're my kind of perfect and even the stars can't look as beautiful as you in my eyes. And the way you love me brings life to my heart every day and helps me to have a fearless love I can't comprehend, but I love it and I love you.

There's not a thing I'd change about you nor replace you with. You're my forever and a forever love is what I share with you, happily and willingly. I feel a peace in my heart because I know you are her, the one, my future wife. So I will love you till forever and ever, and enjoy every moment of it with you.

An Inspired Heart

The Beauty of Your Mind

I'm sorry for seeing your beauty before you.

You're an intelligent girl, you're funny, weird and crazy in a good way and you have a lot going for yourself. Your beauty is a special addition to who you are but it doesn't make you up. So I'm sorry for looking at your beauty more than the things that excite you and cause your mind to want to educate itself.

Like how you love to read and put yourself into the shoes of each character you read about. Like how music is like oxygen to you or how your mind is so creative you can make an amazing piece of art out of scrap.

There's more to you than your beauty and I see that.

Behind the contour, foundation and on fleek eyebrows is a beautiful mind, full of adventure, dreams, goals, aspirations and visions of a future you hope to bring to life. I see that now, so I'm sorry for just seeing your outward appearance. I now see the beauty within you and I think it's beautiful beyond what words could ever describe. And I hope whatever you put that lovely mind to, you accomplish it and your future is brighter than you could ever imagine, that all your dreams come true and everything your heart desires will happen and that your mind remains the most beautiful thing about you.

An Inspired Heart

The Day We Meet

My heart races as my palms get sweaty...

...and breaths get heavy at the thought of meeting you for the first time.

I'm out of my mind. Moments I imagined I'm now able to live and make a reality. And I know as much as I try my best to think of how I'll react when the time comes, I get lost in thought and my mind blacks out as tears fill my eyes. Because I know, in that moment of literally seeing my angel standing in front of me, life will have a whole new meaning and chapter.

You, this person I've been so blessed to get to know and share love with, now wrapped up in my arms, your body pressing against the cage that used to protect you as my rib, the thought blows me away.

I await the day every day that I live for this one moment in time, where for the first time we're in the same place at the same time, face to face and heart to heart.

I'm afraid that I'll never let you go, but I'm comforted in knowing you'll feel the same way, too.

So I will hold you as long as I can, while closing my eyes and allowing this moment to be treasured and imprinted in our hearts, minds and souls. And when I see your face, there's no way I'm looking away, nothing will distract or divert my attention from you. My heart of hearts will be singing a glorious song of love, and happiness will flood my face with a smile that cannot be tamed.

I can't wait, and I'm so excited to one day meet you, the love of my life, for the first time in forever.

.w. that will be one of the best days of my life...

A Little
Random Thought

When I love, I love hard. Like I'll take off my jacket for you and cover you with it just to keep your hair from getting wet, not caring that I only have a t-shirt on. But as long as you're warm and dry, I honestly don't mind getting wet and catching a cold to insure you're ok.

A Broken Heart

I'm Doing My Part

Hear my heart scream! It's calling for you!

Emotionally dehydrated, I need a bottle of your love to hydrate me this instant. I depended on you to give me that love and attention my heart needed to live, but now you've gone, I find myself finding love in the wrong places just to try and fill the hole you've left.

We promised to be each other's umbrella through the storms of life but where are you now?

Pain has polluted the air, causing the rain of problems to sting against my delicate heart. I tried my best to brave this mountain, to keep climbing to the top till we reached the peak of our relationship and could say we made it, that we actually worked as a team, as a unit, as a couple and made it.

But no, the moment you saw something crumble you backed off and left me for dead. I said I couldn't see a life without you and now you're gone.

I'm just alive, not living.

Come back, come fight for what we had, because I will protect and fight for what I love. But if you don't do the same, I guess what we shared wasn't love.

And if it wasn't love, what was it?

A Broken Heart

You Get Me Mad

You make me so angry.

You don't even need to do anything. Just the fact that I love you so much makes me so mad. I just want to scream at you "Love me!!!" Love me so I can love you!

My heart feels so heavy because there's so much love in it and no one to pour it out on. And the thing is, I don't want to pour it out to anyone but you.

You're a ghost to my heart yet you feel so alive in there. I have to fight back tears because I know you aren't worth a single tear falling for you. I lie to myself daily saying I'm over you when I know deep inside I'm far from it. With every heart beat my heart produces more love I wish could be pumped round your body. But no, I'm here, stuck, confused on why my mind still replays times we spent together like an advert in my head.

This pain is unreal because it's emotional but physically hurts.

And when I see you I just want to shoot you down with cupid's arrows and make you fall for me. But then I get mad at make believe things because I use to believe in fantasy but now I leave it all for storybooks.

Like you stress my life out, why are you in my dreams, how are you causing my lungs to take a deep breath at the mention of your name?

I swear I pray to God you get jealous when I find that person that makes me forget about you.

My Little Love Notes...

....

I will happily go down on my two knees to pray that one day I'll find that someone who will have me go down on one knee to make them my life partner...

....

Yes, the man is the head of the house, but the woman is the neck, and without the neck we don't get the support we need to stand up tall and do what we must do as the head...

5th Letter...

Dear Future Wife,

I just thought it would be right to let you know, I'm not perfect.

If my past were a blank canvas, it would not paint such a pretty picture. I mean, I haven't done anything crazy, it's just, I've made plenty of mistakes, but I've gained profitable experience, and that's helped me appreciate and value the small and greater things in life, like you.

I'm telling you this because the past has a way of crawling up like a virus in the form of a person, trying to destroy future progress, because they're either jealous, spiteful or envious of what they see.

One thing I know for sure is I will not let my past mistakes reoccur or hurt you. Whatever you want to know, I will tell. I won't hide anything from you, nor hold back any kind of truth. So if something does pop up, you'll already have the information and not be misled.

I may not know who you are right now, but I value your existence and I will cherish your presence in my life. I will do nothing to hurt you and everything to guard your heart.

I hope from the time I meet you, you would have got this message, so we can both share a blank canvas and paint a new life.

Yours Sincerely,
Amos. C. Pinnock

An Inspired Heart

Love with Faith

Investing love in the wrong person can cause so much pain.

I've invested my time, effort and love into people and ended up in nothing but pain. That pain caused me to lose faith in thinking there is actually someone out there that can love me the way I'll love them, that will make me feel like my time and effort isn't being wasted, but is watering a seed in their heart, helping it produce fruits of love and them happily and willingly sharing that fruit with me.

It came to a point where I honestly thought paying for someone else's mistakes was a normal thing to do, that I'll never receive the same amount of time and effort I give out, that loving will always hurt and I'll spend my days never really being happy but always making others happy.

I lost hope and faith in finding a heart that is compatible with mine, but then you happened, you invaded my vision and caused a crowd of feelings to spring up and rush to see this angelic figure in front of me. You became what my heart wanted to see after every blink, but my mind didn't want to look too much into it because looks can be deceiving. But the moment you spoke, your voice sang to my heart. The more we spoke, my mind took interest and started to realise, your heart is beautiful too.

You put in effort I thought I would never receive, you said kind loving words I thought would never reach my ears, and your actions opened the gates of my heart and started planting seeds of love.

As the seeds you planted grew into fruits, I recognised that everything I thought in the past was wrong. You restored my faith in love and now I have faith in us and in the love we now share.

Thank you.

It might sound weird saying thank you, but I'm grateful that you showed me loving is not a painful but a beautiful thing.

And now I'm going to be faithful in having faith in loving you.

One Night

All I want is one night.

One night just to show you I'm for real, one night to show you that if I could, I would place you amongst the stars because that's how beautiful you are. One night to drop you home, walk to your door and feel accomplished that I got you safely inside, not me being inside of you. Just one night, a night where we'll forget we have control of our legs as they walk us for hours, while talking about your interests and hobbies, your favourite and worst foods, things that make you laugh and things that make you cry.

Give me one night.

With that night I'll show you how I find your heart so much more beautiful than your body. I want to see you laugh rather than strip, I want to see your eyes glow up with happiness rather than the size of your hips. Just give me one night and I'll show you this is not just an act, but my lifestyle, that my mother raised me this way and I'm not playing a player's game. You're a princess and I can see the Queen in your eyes. And with my heart, I promise you I'm not flooding your mind with lies.

So as the moon's bright and the stars shine…

…give me one night to show you we can be together for a lifetime.

An Inspired Heart

Crazy in Love

Let's love like we're stupid.

Let's annoy the impossible till it allows us to access its hidden treasures. Let's love in public, holding hands in the park, hold-each other in the middle of town, and take selfies with random and weird faces.

Let's announce our love, let's find the highest building, and on the balcony of the top floor we'll scream and profess our love for one another for the whole city to hear.

Let's shame negative minds and show them love is not hard or a burden. When you find and love the right person, love is calm but wild, crazy and fun that brings happiness and tears of joy.

Let's make our lifestyle a testimony of how beautiful love is when you invest God, faith and hope in it. Yes, we may go rough patches, but love is always that antidote that cures the disease of pain, hurt, discomfort and confusion, plus keeping the promise we once made never to rest our heads until our hearts are at peace with each other.

So baby, let's love like we're the only two people in the world. I'm crazy about you and you're crazy about me making us crazy in love.

Let's never stop loving, as love never stops loving us.

.w. lets never hold back on love...

An Inspired Heart

Trust Me to Love You

Let me touch your heart and kiss it with my lips of love.

And let me take your hand and hold it tight. I'll guide you as we take our first steps of walking in love. All I ask is that you trust me, I've been waiting all my life to make this move.

Dreams haven't felt so close now I've found you. I won't scar your heart, I won't let go and leave you confused and alone. I'll be right next to you the whole time. Home has been found in each other's hearts, so don't ever let me go. Love has been found in the happiness we share and I've found my life in your heart. Fearlessly I'll give my all to you. I find it dangerous not to, because I don't ever want to lose you.

I've made up in my mind that there's not a soul in this universe I would rather spend time loving with a million heartbeats. You'll never know how much sharing a life with you means to me, because it'll take me a life time to explain how precious, treasured and vital you are to me.

With each day oxygen passes through our body, I will crown you with my love and make you Queen of my heart.

A Little
Random Thought

It's her heart, I see it, it holds a treasure of love that is so precious to her she can't help but protect it. It's all she has, and she awaits the day she finds someone who actually loves her so much, their love resembles a key that unlocks her heart, allowing her to happily and fearlessly share her treasure of her love for him...

Snow Angel

Snow, I'll call you snow.

    I love to watch the snowfall at night, while it covers the floor and looks like the wings of an angel. A snow angel, fallen from the sky to grace the earth with your beauty.

    Whoever beholds you a warm peace shelters their heart and lifts a smile on their face. Speechless and overwhelmed with emotions, eyebrows raise as heavy breaths follow, eyes slowly close as words are swallowed.

    Why?

    Because in order to describe this beautiful splendour in front of me I'll have to take a dictionary from heaven because no words on this earth will do you justice.

    All I can do is stare, at you, my snow angel, stare until my eyes water and sting, stare until my mind paints this image of you on the canvas of my heart, so every time I close my eyes I can view it like I've never blinked.

    My snow angel, every day with you feels like Christmas, joy bells ring as heaven's angels sing. I thank God for the happiness you bring. And as your snow of love settles in my heart, no matter how heated life will get, the love will never melt away and the snow of love will never stop falling.

    I'll forever be falling for you, my Snow Angel.

An Inspired Heart

Ezbie

Distance brought us closer.

At times I thought we would never be, but two have become one because of the distance that separated you from me. Our hearts always stayed in touched even though our minds wandered and searched in different places to replace the memories and thoughts of each other we thought scared our hearts.

You went and did your own thing and so did I. Eyes wandered but inside, our hearts stood still, patiently waiting to reunite with each other.

It makes sense why every other relationship failed, because no matter how much I tried to put my heart into them, it refused to give away a love that was made for you and only you. And as time went by and days became months and months years, I felt stuck in the past, because my heart was still in the years we had spent together, never letting go or forgetting, but bringing them alive every time I closed my eyes.

I couldn't get over you.

No matter how much I tried, you wouldn't leave my heart. I swore I'd never go back to you because the pain you caused left me at an all-time low. But the low brought me to my knees, my knees brought me to God and God brought me back to you. And now here we are, seeing eternity in each other eyes, hearts reunited and minds no longer divided and both thinking about the future we now share together.

Our distance brought us closer and made our love stronger. Now with no doubt and no fear, I know forever you are here.

.w. I'm so glad love never gave up on us...

You Next to Me

It's nights like these I think about you...

...nights where I wish I could turn my head and see you laying right next to me in the stillness of the night. Just to hear you breathe and feel your heartbeat against my ear as I rest my head on your chest. Then there's that beautiful warmth we create as we lay lie next to each other, and the only time we move is to hold each other tighter.

It's nights like these I wish we could clear our minds of every thought and just listen to the peace the surrounds us. Each night we'll pray for each other and life, we'll exchange the words *I love you* before our eyes set and fall asleep. Each night we'll fall asleep happy knowing we'll be waking up to each other and exchange our first good mornings with each other as our eyes open.

I long for these times to come, I can't wait to just look over and see your head on a pillow next to mine and thank God that I'm with the love of my life. I can't wait; I honestly can't wait. I could wake up and fall asleep to your face every morning and still get excited and overwhelmed with happiness that I've got you in my life forever, and that a day or night won't go by without my eyes seeing your beautiful face as the last thing at night and first thing in the morning.

An Inspired Heart

A Fight for Love

Shoot me now or forever hold your peace.

Because only death will part my love from you. You can't push me away, you can't push my love away and I will love you till the end of time.

The space you try create between us out of the fear past pains inflicted on you will not scare me nor cause me to stop loving you. I will fight this fear you have of you loving with your heart and get you where I am, and that is being afraid not to love you with all you have.

But if loving you means giving you the space and time you need to get over the fear of free-falling in love, I will happily love you in silence, only speaking when needed and being there when you're in need of comfort. I will try my very best to help you and be there for you. Just don't ever forget each and every word that is exhaled out of my heart then spoken to you is true.

I understand it might take you a while to get over this fear of being hurt again once you've opened up your heart. I understand you're pushing me away cause you're afraid you might hurt me, but seeing your heart broken only makes me want to help you search for the broken pieces and put it back together again.

I promise the love I'll show to you will be the cement that keeps your heart in one piece.

I won't give up.

I love you; what I love I will fight for. And no matter how many times you may hurt me in the process, I'm will come back and fight until you love me as I love you.

.w. you are worth the fight...

Girl You Deserve the Best

It hurts me to see your cheeks shrink as your smile fades away from your face.

You're done with talking because it seems like you're going around in circles about the same thing, and even though you want to talk, words refuse to leave your mouth and tears start to fall.

Tears should never fall the way they fall from your face. They fall as if to say *why does loving him hurt, why does he not appreciate me and see my value? I give my all but he minimises me and focuses on himself and other things.*

Plus the more you try and put effort in, the more you get hurt. It hurts me to see this, it hurts to see a diamond get thrown around instead of polished, kept well, looked after, and valued in the eye of its beholder.

You have to free yourself from his painful grip on your heart.

Yes, you deserve better and yes, you are better than him. Open the eyes of your heart and see you are beautiful, you are to be loved like you're the only female in the world, that you are a unique and a precious person who deserves nothing but the best presented and given to you. Don't settle for less, because when God made you he said you are fearfully and wonderfully made, meaning even in his eyes you are precious and greatly valued. You are a Princess waiting to be crowned Queen.

So sit on the throne of your heart and do all you can to protect and rule it with confidence in knowing…

…you deserve the very best and should be treated like the best.

My Little Love Notes...

If someone moves on, it's not because they didn't love you; sometimes it's because you pushed them so far away they had no choice but to move on...

At times we may think that our strength is found in holding on, but sometimes our true strength is found in letting go...

A Broken Heart

I'm Letting You Go So I Can Be Loved

I did try.

I tried to open your eyes and show you that I am for real. You knew by the effort I put in I would literally do anything for you and you took advantage of that. I never even noticed until the love I gave out started to hurt, then I started to question. *Are we for real or are we all in my head and in reality it's just me.*

All the happy times were all in my head. You never even showed or indicated any sign that you were interested or even felt the same way. My love vouched for you in all the places you lacked, my love made me blind to the fact that I loved the concept of you and not you, and that's why I kept you around and never noticed you didn't show any love.

I guess I just wanted to love someone so much, I didn't mind who it was.

Or even if they gave the same efforts I did.

I just wanted somebody to love.

I could blame myself but at the same time you just kept on receiving while not even trying to give. This is not what I deserve, I deserve to reap the harvest of love I've sown in someone.

So now, I will love with my eyes open and only give my all to someone who's more than happy to give their all to me. I'm letting you go and moving on.

Onto someone who loves me as much as I love them.

An Inspired Heart

A Consistent Love

You loved me at my lowest.

You saw me angry and never judged my actions but gave me space and understood it was for a moment. You waited, waited till I calmed down then laid my head on your chest, and rested your lips on my forehead as each heartbeat told me *baby, it's going to be ok.*

You stood by me when I had lost hope in myself. With your hands wrapped around mine you insisted we prayed a prayer of thanks; thanks for life and the blessing of being able to see another day; thanks for how far we've come and where we are going to go.

Each time you stared into my eyes and uttered the words I love you, you energised my heart and gave me strength I never knew was there. You have fulfilled Genesis 2:18.

There hasn't been a sunrise or sunset where you haven't helped me through life, in highs and lows you've not only been my love but my friend, best friend and hero. You built a smile on my face from the wreckage of a broken heart and you believed in my dreams when I gave up and refused to sleep. Your consistency showed me your love was real and I love you for displaying the love of God.

I will be here for you in the same way. You have not only shown me, but helped me know how to truly love someone.

And that someone for me is you.

.w. for that I will never stop loving you...

I'm Happy to Love You

My heart will always lead me to you.

How?

Well, it starts to race when it senses you are near. Nature whispers your name as a constant reminder that you are the one. The sun becomes your spotlight whenever you're in front of me and the moon becomes our lamp when the sky is at its darkest.

All signs of an everlasting love buried in the heart of a female, points to you, my wonder woman, my Princess, my dream girl, my rib, my heart. I see my world in your eyes, I see my happiness in your smile, I feel love in your kiss and peace in your embrace.

I no longer feel cold in the winter because your arms are my blankets.

Tomorrow seems to never come because every day feels like a dream with you that I don't want to wake up from. I find it amazing loving you because it brings me joy, it's not a job nor a chore because I know I'm loving the right person. So with all the strength in my heart I will love you.

I will love you for life.

I Want to Hear From You

It hurts not hearing from you.

Every hour I'm staring at my phone, hoping that every text I receive is from you. I wish I just knew where you were just so I can tell you how much I miss you and hold you like I haven't seen you in years.

I'm not stalking you, it's just I'm not use to any day going by without hearing from you. It's like you've become my heart's oxygen; it can't beat without you.

So please, pick up your phone and check your messages. If your busy, let me know so I know that you'll soon be back.

Your absence brings a loneliness I'm not use to. It hurts, and I start to over-think things to the point where my mind feels like it's going to explode with thoughts. I don't like it. I don't like you ever being away. I'm not crazy, it's just that I don't have anyone else to feel this way about. There's no one I could miss in a way that brings pain.

So, I can't wait to hear from you so your presence and soft kind words can take away this pain.

A Little
Random Thought

Distance made him realise his love for her was deeper than he had imagined, so he continued to wait for her hoping that one day they'll look back at the distance and appreciate how close it made them...

6th Letter...

Dear Future Wife

I'm waiting. I am waiting, for you.
 No matter how many girls try to pose as you, or even try to wear your title, I know they're not you. Even though I don't know who you are, something in me knows that they aren't you. They don't send the same tingle down my spine the way you do, they don't have me smiling so hard it hurts my cheeks like you do.
 Only you can cause my heart to pound and send a ripple of love around my body. Might sound crazy cause I know not who you are, but I love being committed to you. I love knowing I will have no more ex's. The search for the second half of my heart will be over, because when I find you, that'll be it. You'll forever be in my life. You'll be the 50 to my 50 making us 100, completing me totally.
 I've never really been a patient guy. I've found it hard to wait for most of the things in my life. But the good book says, "Good things come to those who wait." I disagree but agree. You're more than good to me. You're beyond amazing, a masterpiece yet to be placed as the centrepiece in my heart. So I will be patient and wait. And while I'm waiting I hope you find this message, so the wait will soon be over.

Yours Sincerely,
Amos. C. Pinnock

An Inspired Heart

Just Me and You

I promise I'll hold you and you can tell me when to let go. I'll kiss you every day till the day we get old.

We can be emotional together and stare into each other's eyes as happiness floods our soul.

Dance with me to a thousand love songs, get lost with me in emotions and get found in love.

Lay next to me. Let's cuddle till our eyes get heavy and sleep kidnaps us.

Dream with me of a whole new world where all of our heart's desires come true. Then let's wake up together, and watch the sunrise as it paints the sky with its beauty.

Love me as I love you. Take my hand. Let's take a step together into a place where's there's no broken promises, no broken hearts and no pain. All that matters is what we have, so let's protect each other and always be true to one another. And from this day forward…

…I promise I'll hold you and you can tell me when to let go. I'll kiss you every day till the day we get old.

.w. let's do this forever…

I'll See You Soon

Just because you're no longer alive on earth doesn't stop you from existing in my heart.

Your eyes may be closed forever but mine close too, and when they close, I see you. People will call it dreaming but I say it's another chance in another life, where the seconds, minutes and hours we never got to spend together get added up so we can have them with each other.

And yes there's a physical distance between us but your spirit still lives on, in me and everyone you inspired, loved and cared for. Your kindness, your contributions, the smiles you put on people's faces, and the hope and life you gave to those in need has built a statue of you in all the hearts you touched. Thank you for being an amazing figure of love in my life. This isn't good bye, this is see you soon.

I Love you.

An Inspired Heart

Inside Love

True love loves in ways we would call mysterious...

...but when we come to terms with the fact that love is never really meant to be understood, just done whole heartedly, we inhabit and inherit true love. Love is a force that moves and freely, it has no limit nor end, it's loud but humble with distinctive actions and comforting in words.

It calls our reality fake and our fantasy reality, because our reality tends to come with chains of limits and love is limitless. Our fantasy is a world full of possibility and love is full of possibility.

Love can encourage, it brings unity and destroys division. It helps you believe and it busts confidence. Love is a positive and always has a beautiful end to the life of those who share true love. It's neither a myth nor fairy tale.

It is as real as you and I.

A Little
Random Thought

Guys have feelings too, and some of you girls need to stop breaking these good guy's hearts just because once upon a time, you decided to go for someone who didn't know how to treat you good…

A Broken Heart

A Wish and A Hate

I wish I had never met you.

If I knew I would have fallen for you so hard, I would have kept a friendly distance away from you and left it at that. Because it hurts, I love you so much. I honestly can't stop thinking about you.

Your smile that shines a sun in my heart, your accent, how beautiful you are. The way you touch my hands, the way you look into my eyes and unlock my heart, the magical time we spent together... I would wish them all away if it takes away all of this pain. I'm sorry to say but it's true.

I'm not supposed to be afraid to love. Love's not supposed to hurt this bad.

I don't like loving alone. I hate not knowing how you feel, I hate you being so calm around me when daily I wish just to be by your side. I hate you not even hinting you still love me. I hate the fact it seems like you're over me. I hate that I can't move on, I hate that I wish every happy moment I spent was spent with you. I hate how I want to go out and buy you things just to see your face light up.

I hate one way loving.

I hate having the faith that one day we'll get back together. As much as I want us to, I have to not give myself hope, because I don't want to get hurt again.

One thing I do wish though, is I wish I could fall asleep, then open my eyes and it'll all be over. No more pain or heartaches; loving you as a friend.

And that is all.

A Broken Heart

The Pain of Distance

I wish the oceans were as small as I they seem on a classroom globe...

...then I would be able to take a few steps and be right next to you.

Missing you has been so painful, the fact that time doesn't lend time for us to spend time together makes me hate every clock I see.

I'm not conscious of the distance between us when we talk, because we talk ourselves out of reality into our own world. And in the world of conversations, you're right next to me, but the moment you leave and the feeling of missing you kicks in, reality opens the eyes of my heart and distance becomes a horrible monster.

I know we chose this. No one said it would be easy. I fully understand that, but regardless of distance I promise you no matter how far you are, as long as God authorises breath in me, as oxygen pushes blood around my body enabling my heart to beat, each beat will represent my love for you living on.

But there's one thing I ask from you: help me become blind to this distance. I don't want to face the reality that you're thousands of miles away. I will do all I can to make you feel I'm as close as roots are to soil. Do the same for me, because this distance between us is painful.

But I know your love. Spare time and effort will be a drug that would numb the pain.

A Broken Heart

You Matter to Me

Seven billion people on this earth and you, you've captured my heart.

Before I would find it so easy to move on, but you, you've caused me to be stuck, stuck in a void. When I look through the eyes of my heart all I see is you. No other girl matters; time with any other girl seems pointless because all my arrows point to you.

Distracted by the lack of attention you show me I replay the memories we share over and over in my head, and I've come to realise after lying to myself the truth is, you're all I want.

The more I want to move on, the closer I get to you. Closure won't help because I'm open to letting you in whenever you like. I'm so sure you're the one and there's no other numbers except for you.

You're my one and only.

If wishing on a star was real, I'd wish on all of them that we can spend a lifetime together. And every moment spent together is print screened in the photo album in our hearts, so if there's a distance between us I can go through them and allow my imagination to relive them, making your absence unknown. You've finished my journey for seeking the one. I just hope somewhere in your heart you feel the same way to.

A Little
Random Thought

I'm glad every other relationship failed and I'm glad I got rejected, because rejections led me to you and failure had me appreciate the success in our relationship...

7th Letter...

Dear Future Wife,

I'm so excited for the endless time we'll spend together.

Long walks as we hold hands, fingers link and thumbs stroke against each other. Nights under a cloud of stars, pointing out which one led me to you. Wining and dining at different restaurants, forgetting every diet we put ourselves on. Long talks exchanging dreams, visions, memories, thoughts, ideas, goals and emotions. Living, loving and capturing every moment like it's our last while creating a memory bank only we can access. Movie nights with popcorn fights, double dates with close mates.

Day and night prayers to God our father, studying, quoting and reading the word to show ourselves approved. Keeping God as the centre of our life so we can be prosperous and successful in all we do.

We'll be living the dreams we once dreamt.

Pursuing happiness won't be hard because we'll personally deliver it into each other's hearts daily. I hope you find this message so we can take these imagined moments and make them come to life.

Yours Sincerely,
Amos. C. Pinnock

An Inspired Heart

My Miracle

You're my Miracle.

From the moment I saw you I fell madly in love. Oceans of happiness flooded my life and washed me upon the shores of stars where dreams and wishes come true.

I can't help but forever be amazed that you are mine. I don't think you'll ever understand how I feel, that you, a girl made from the wings of angels, is with someone simple like me.

Your smile inspires God to create, the stars bow to the sparkle in your eyes and your kiss gives me life.

How, oh how am I with someone like you?

I could only dream a dream that dreamt about being with you, it was that hard to imagine someone like me being with a diamond rose like you. Blessed is an understatement; finding the words is impossible but the only word I can use to explain what you are to me is *Miracle*. A one in a billion gift from God that I cherish and honour with everything within me.

You, you are my Miracle.

.w. I will never take you for granted...

Perfect Beauty

You are beautiful!

There aren't any stars in the sky that can shine as beautiful as you do. Don't follow the media and the image they print on people; you are to be followed. The unique beauty you have could inspire the very mind of Shakespeare and cause him to write a story about you called "The Beauty of a Thousand Angels."

Gazing into your eyes has never been so peaceful as my heart whispers to me *behold the truth of untouched beauty*.

Make up has to change its name when placed on you because it can't enhance what's already perfect; nothing needs to be added or changed.

So excuse me while I boast to the entire world about you. I'm not just honoured but humbled and grateful to the Almighty that He has blessed me to be in love with a perfectly crafted jewel.

The beautiful thing about you is your heart makes up one hundred percent of your beauty. I believe the state of one's heart reflects their whole image, and because you have a heart that beats compassion, love and kindness, in the eyes of the beholder, beauty is so plain and clear to see. With that being said I am forever grateful to God. I have been blessed to have someone who has been shaped and moulded from the clouds of heaven.

My Little Love Notes...

His heart broke when he realised the fight he put into loving her wasn't enough...

I take my heart out to battle every day; to fight for you in hope that one day we'll find peace in love and not war...

A Broken Heart

Story Behind a Tear

Fallen.

Memories of you are like a hammer that breaks the knees of my strength and causes me to bow to a tear. Broken promises like shattered glass that has cut through my heart.

I used to have a treasure under my chest, but now that's gone. I'm but a lonely pirate sailing the seas of love I thought we would dive into together.

I used to think my all wasn't enough, but the truth is you're not enough for my all.

Every day a river of questions flows out of me; heated by anger it evaporates and creates a cloud of prayers.

God, where did I go wrong? Did I give her a part of my heart that was meant to be reserved for another? Why is my past with her a ghost stalking my present?

Memories and moments we shared stain locations we visited, leaving a scent that reminds me of her. Our stars never aligned so I guess it was the wrong timing for us to make a connection.

To be, or not to be? A question that disables my very ability to move on. And until I get an answer that births closure, memories of you weaken my knees, causing me to bow to a tear.

Heart Under Oath

If I could live without a heart I would.

Not forever, just until I miss it, because right now I want to throw it away or even lock it away so far and bury it so deep I can't hear it beat.

It's lustful call for love seduces my emotions and makes me open up quick, trust easy and love hard at anyone who tells me what I think I want to hear. Its desire blinds my common sense and makes me believe in a world full of fantasy and dreams, where true love is easy to access if you give all you have straight away. Never learning patience it's constantly rushing and racing instead of pacing itself, taking things slow, or getting to know the person before falling head over heels for them. It hurts me and leaves me an emotional wreck because too many times have I listened to my heart thinking *this time this person could be different from the rest*!

So I go full speed ahead giving it my all only to find myself crashing into the same wall of hurt, pain and regret. And when my heart is down, common-sense asks me *when will you learn that you need to burn the rope your heart has around the neck of your emotions, pulling you from relationship to relationship, and start thinking with your head not heart?*

Now is that time.

No longer will my heart have a say until common sense gives it permission to speak. It will no longer dictate my movements.

I will be the ruler of my emotions.

A Broken Heart

I Can See You See Me

No straight face can hide your pain.

When your mouth is closed your eyes speak.

I hurt you by not loving myself. All you wanted me to see is that I am special; I am not a product shaped by society but a masterpiece modelled by the hands of God. I allowed opinions and false statements to influence how I acted and ran my life.

You tried to show me that I am beautiful, loved and noticed even without the amount of followers, likes or Re-Tweets I can get off Instagram or Twitter.

In your eyes, I saw that you saw me. You saw my flaws, my imperfections, my insecurities.

But regardless of all of that, you loved me.

You loved me so hard there came a time where your love destroyed the cage my problems put me in and allowed me to be free. I was free, free to be me, weird, crazy, funny and serious. You took me on - in your life, in your arms and in your heart, and even though at times insecurities or past pains crept up and bit me, causing me to push you away, you never held back your love, but gave me space and time to breath and vent, never judging me but encouraging me and never letting me forget you care and were there for me. All of what you've done demonstrated true love, and I don't want to lose you, because you have become the one I want and need to love.

Forgive me for allowing my pain to hurt you. All I ask of you now is to let me love you with everything within me.

As you have done to and for me.

A Broken Heart

Exit Out of My Heart

I rescheduled my life for you...

...broke down and reconstructed walls for you. You could call me a wizard the way I created conversations out of the silent air you breathed when with me.

The way I struggled to find reasons in your empty box of emotion, you could call it self-pleasure because my mind would make things up to justify you.

I would call your name, you would turn your head and look at me and I could tell you lacked respectful attention with that dead stare. Your eyes might as well have been closed, because eyes don't lie and I could see yours were full of them.

You were basically a vampire to my emotions; you stuck your fangs into the neck of my heart and drained all the love out of me. Your presence was darkness to my heart and the only way to make a vampire flee is to bring it into the light.

So let me shine some light on my heart's housekeeping rules. To your left, right, front and back are fire exit signs. I am setting fire to this relationship so please could you exit as soon as possible before you get burnt?

Thank you for your cooperation.

A Little
Random Thought

Be with someone who motivates you to be better, inspires you to create, takes your mind on adventures so you can explore, is loyal so you can commit, loves your imperfections so you'll always feel beautiful, and guards your heart so you won't be afraid to love...

An Inspired Heart

Know Your Worth

I saw your heart and that's what made me fall for you.

I saw passion in your eyes but humility in your stature. I saw hesitation in your approach–but confidence in your delivery. I saw beauty on your exterior and love on the interior. I feel as if I saw the real you.

I saw a girl that had a dream and would do all she could to birth it out of the womb of her mind and bring it to life. I saw a girl that was so selfless, she would happily help out others when in need and wouldn't mind if she went without because she knew sacrifice is the ultimate example of love. I saw the prayers of her mother help shape and build her into a unique and elegant lady that had the faith to move mountains. I saw the reason why God looked at Adam and said *man should not be alone.*

I saw you.

And you need to see you.

So that no matter what obstacles in life you face, they won't weigh you down and misshape the great, unique and amazing person you are. So that sticks and stones won't break your bones and the names, nonsense and negative words people like to speak won't hurt you because you know your worth and you won't settle for less than you deserve.

Walk in your worth and don't ever lose sight of the princess you are and the Queen you're going to become.

An Inspired Heart

To My Mother

Mom, I love you

My heart and I are so glad you are the first woman we loved. My soul and I are so grateful that God has blessed us to be the child of an absolutely amazing woman. My Queen, my personal guardian angel, thank you for teaching and showing me how to love, so when I have my own wife and children, the seeds of love you once planted in me would have brought forth beautiful fruits containing happiness, joy, peace, and love.

Thank you for being a cornerstone for me to lean on when I couldn't stand on my own two feet. You supported me, looked out for me, guided me and had my back when no one else did.

Thank you for loving God.

I say thank you because the way you love Him helped me love Him, and the way He loved you helped me see He loves me too. Thank you for your prayers in the early A.M and the late P.M. I know for a fact if it wasn't for those prayers I would have been in a broken state.

Because when I couldn't pray for myself you did, no matter how big I got, spiritually, you held me up like a baby before God and offered me as a living sacrifice, and for that I am grateful.

I love you more than words can comprehend.

Thank you for not only being my Mom, but a Mother too.

A Lookout

Where are you?

I know you're somewhere in this world but where? I want to talk to you! I have so many things I want to tell you, so much I want to show you and an incomprehensible amount of love I want to give to you.

Where are you?! People say wait and she'll come but I always find myself waiting in the wrong arms of the wrong person. I don't want my loneliness to be comforted by someone. I'm done with pointless relationships, my heart is dying to find you, and I've got all of these false advertisements coming in and out of my life claiming they are the one, but I'm like *no*!

The one is the name of that unique individual that you can only find once in a lifetime. I can't get over the fact that you are anonymous and it's killing me not knowing at least your name. I pray to God you're closer than I think because my heart is impregnated with love you for, and it's ready to birth out and share this precious gift with you.

Don't be shy to approach or pop up to me. I'll welcome you with open arms and give you a love that is limitless and will never die out on you. Just let me know who you are.

Bring this search of finding the one to an end.

.w. I can't wait for the day we finally meet...

My
Little Love
Notes...

When someone really matters to you, showing them you care is not a tiring thing, but something you enjoy and look forward to doing...

Find that person who makes falling in love an enjoyable and wonderful thing to experience...

A Broken Heart

Let's Make Us Happen

It hurts me not to love you with all I have.

There's literally no one on the face of this earth I want to love but you. People spend their whole life trying to find someone to love... true love.

I felt like I found you and you found me, but why do we allow distance to separate what we have? I said I'll be happy for you if you find someone closer to you that'll love you and take care of you, but deep down I'll be broken and destroyed inside.

I hate how tears create a swamp on my pillow at night. I hate thinking about what we could have been if only we went the extra mile. But now we're stuck here; where here is I don't know, but I hate where we are.

I want us to be.

I want our love to reunite and bring peace to the cry of our tears.

Let's make us happen, let's not allow distance to be a wall that separates us. Let's make a way for our hearts to connect again and rest in each other's arms.

I will do all I can because all I want to do is love you.

A Broken Heart

I Want to Feel Loved Too

I want to get sucked into the black hole of your pupil and get lost in the stars of your love while you stare at me.

    I want you to tell me you love me and that when you're with me, there's no one else you'd rather be with. I want to feel your hands play with the hairs on the back of my neck and each time your fingers surf on my skin, I want to feel a wave of goosebumps travel down my body. I want to be surprised with random kisses on my cheeks, head and lips. I want my head to rest on your chest and cuddle in peace as our heartbeats sing to us. I want to know I'm valued in your life, that you're here for me, and you'll do anything to make me happy. I want your hands to hold mine as we walk in the sun, rain and snow. I want to be on your Instagram for all to see that I'm yours and you're mine.

    I'm tired of doing these things alone. I just really want that person who will do the same for me as I for them. I just want to feel loved, like I matter, like I mean something to someone...

    ...to you!

A Real Goodbye

I'm only saying goodbye because I love you.

Now this goodbye is for real. There's no one last hug, no one last kiss, there's no looking back. Because if I do those things, physically I would have walked away but mentally I would have stayed.

So no!

No last words declaring how true and real my love is towards you with a hidden intention to make you think this isn't really goodbye. No last minute texts with hearts and kisses, no gifts to symbolise and represent a part of me forever with you, nothing! I'm not leaving anything behind to give myself a reason to come back to you just to see your face and be in your presence one last time. Not even a footprint so you can trace my steps back to me.

If someone truly loves you, you can let them go and they'll come back. If it was meant to be, somewhere and somehow in time, our paths will cross because destiny will lead us back together, showing us the love we once shared was true and it never disappeared but hibernated in the cocoon of our hearts.

I believe everything happens for a reason, so if you were just for a season in my life, I'm glad the seasonal love we shared both helped and taught us lessons for whatever's to come in the future. But until we know for sure...

...this is goodbye.

My
Little Love
Notes...

....

Forever is our destination and each day, with every heartbeat, you will be the one I share it with...

....

Today I will love you like there's no tomorrow; tomorrow I will love more than yesterday and every moment leading to our future, I promise, a day won't go by where I hold back love from you...

An Inspired Heart

Like it's Our Last Time

I really don't know when our last time is.

So promise me you'll hold me like this is the last day on earth. Kiss me like there's no tomorrow, tell me how much you love me.

The present is a gift, so let's unwrap it and take advantage of it. Let's give our all into making each other happy, let's make a beautiful world where all that exists is us. Let our tears of joy create an ocean and our love be an island, our happiness will be the sun and words of affection the food that never leaves us hungry.

We will never leave anything unsaid or allow fear to shrink our confidence in each other.

And before we close our eyes our love for each other will go up in a prayer to the Almighty, asking Him to grace us with another day that we can spend and share together.

But until our eyes set with the sun on another day, each morning we rise our love will be a testimony to how we exchanged our present as a gift to one another, so we can both cherish the time we have in each other's arms.

An Inspired Heart

I Never Stopped Liking You

All I can do is hope... hope that we could be something.

Now these thoughts are supposed to be unknown, but I'm finding it hard not to let you know that I've never stopped liking you.

If I was ever to see you in person I'd drop whatever I'm doing, run over to you with my arms wide open and hold you like a free man holding his loved ones after 10 years of being locked away in prison.

What if has become a stalker to my thoughts. *What if* you two had given it a try? *What if* you waited for her? *What if* you had one more chance?

I know for sure the palms of my hands would have become a pillow your heart could have rested on as I held it knowing I'll never do anything to hurt or abuse it.

The first time we met up I saw heaven in your eyes and it felt like paradise when you were in my arms. At that moment my heart started to construct and build a place for you in me, because I'd never thought someone who radiates beauty could ever enter my life. It's like you hopped out of my dreams and became real. You're the Lioness to my Lion heart, you made it go wild with emotions to the point where I had to tranquilise and put it to sleep.

That Lion still lives, waiting to kill *what if* with his Lioness, hoping this time she is here to stay.

Time With You

Pull me in close and whisper into my ear the words *I love you...*

...so those three words travel down the ladder of my neck, across the bridge of my collarbone, then through the gates of my ribcage and make camp on the pillows of my heart.

Every time you hold my hand and rub your thumb against my skin you send a swarm of butterflies straight to my stomach. Each time I hold you, my eyes close and body goes into a trance, so I'm not conscious of what's around me, but only what's in front of me.

The mere fact that I'm holding my second half brings a comfort that raises my body temperature and makes me feel like I'm sitting next to a fire on a cold winter's night.

I love the way your cheeks rise, eyes glow and nose scrunches when you smile. I love it when your smell lingers on my clothes, because whenever I inhale it, it's an anaesthesia that causes me to daydream about you and relieves the pain missing you brings.

I await the days where there aren't any days that go by without spending time with you.

Just to look down into your eyes as my hand is placed under your chin, tilting your head up as I tilt mine down to have our lips make a connection that sends a pulse of love directly to your heart. Just to fall asleep and wake up to a gift of love formed in a human body just for me. I'll never get bored of seeing or being with you.

Why?

Because every day with you is a new adventure in life ready to be explored, and even though I've found my treasure in you, daily we can both create moments to treasure together.

8th Letter...

Dear Future Wife,

It's Valentine's Day.
    There hasn't been a single moment leading up to this day where I haven't thought of how I'd pamper you from the AM till PM. I'll treat this day like it's an event planned just for you.
    You'll wake up to a breakfast that will satisfy your taste buds. A beautiful warm bath surrounded with white and red rose petals, while candles leave a beautiful scent with a glass of your favourite wine on the side waiting for you after you finish your breakfast. I would go on but the rest of the day is a surprise so I won't say any more.
    But I'm so excited, I cannot wait for the adventures following this day.
    Just to see your smile sustained, your eyes sparkle and speck when you're speechless, I'll constantly be staring over at you thanking God I'm finally spending Valentine's Day with the love of my life. Year after year I'll make sure the 24 hours of that day your heart will be on fire with love.
    Yes, every day I will treat you as the Queen of my heart, but that day, expect to feel like it was made for you. You're my Valentine for life, so I hope you find this message so you can prepare yourself to be ambushed with love.

Yours Sincerely,
Amos. C. Pinnock

A Little
Random Thought

I love warm tight hugs, the kind of hugs where in the seconds I'm holding you, I forget about everything around me. The kind of hugs where your scent is left on my clothes, so every time I think about you, I just grab a piece of clothing and relive that moment in my head...

An Inspired Heart

Cuddling

I just want to cuddle.
    Nothing sexual, my hands won't slide into places that will mess up or heat up this moment. Sorry if I'm being blunt, it's just I want to hold you, I want to have my feet up on the sofa as you have yours up while your head rests on my chest. Our eyes may be locked on whatever movie we'll be watching, but at random times I know I'll look down at you and smile with the thoughts *I love this girl* running through my mind while I apply kisses to your head at the most random times.
    I literally just want to feel your body against mine, not feel me inside of you, but hold you like how I hold my pillows when I'm feeling lonely at night. Just to have you in my embrace, my arms around your waist and your skin pressed against my face would be just perfect. You don't even have to talk much. Just hearing you breathe is enough for me. My fingers will be sliding through your hair as you doze off to sleep, then I'll give you one last kiss as I fall asleep to the thoughts that this was a beautiful night.
    So baby all I want to do is cuddle, not just with anybody, but with you.

.w. you can tell me when to let go...

You are Happiness

Your happiness is beautiful.

The unique smile you possess can persuade a bad day it's good. The joy that is carried in the womb of your heart cannot be understood by mortal minds, for when darkness seems to creep in like a thief in the night in your life, you are not afraid. You manage to dissect the negativity out of the darkness and inject positive fluids that cause the darkness to shrivel up and die.

I love the fact that you give small things a big value, like how you get excited over simple achievements because you know no matter how small the achievement is, it can have a big impact. You pull out the greatness in everyone you come across and push down insecurities of those who are broken and hurt.

A beautiful masterpiece are the words I use to describe your personality and mind. You are a gift of happiness to all you meet and I'm glad I've been blessed to have met you.

An Inspired Heart

Forever With You

Forever and a day is my mission...

...a mission to love you and never stop. It's my aim, my goal, a passion that will never die out and will always be for you.

Stars fall from the sky to crown you Queen of my love. The sun stood still in the sky and even though it was time for it to set, it stared and watched you as you shone with beauty. Warm winds gathered, flowers bloomed and trees stood tall just to show respect to you. Even the earth knows how amazing and precious you are, how beautiful, stunning and elegant you are when eyes behold you.

I cannot and will not take for granted you being in my life. I see and understand that there is no other person in this world like you. This is why my love for you will be unique, no other person will give you love or feelings you don't get from me, because I will give you my all, I will put in and give you my best, the very best love my heart, mind, body and soul can give.

I see you for you, and love you for you and I know you are one of a kind

And will love you now, forever and always.

9th Letter...

Dear Future Wife,

No matter what, I'll be here for you.

A day won't go by where you'll feel like I'm absent from your life. I will make it my mission that whenever I'm not physically present, my love will be a blanket that warms you up from the cold feeling of loneliness. You won't have to worry about my location in the early AM, because every night I will be by your side. I will not disappear if we ever fight; that same night we'll spend time fixing the broken pieces of our heart insuring that everything is all right between us.

When you're ill I'll be there to cater to your every need even if it means I have to take time off because you can't cater for yourself. My chest will be a pillow when you want to rest your head. My ears are open 24 hours a day, listening to you laugh, complain, vent or let out whatever is on your mind. My hands are here for you to hold and I'll be a shoulder to lean on.

No matter what, I'm here for you, supporting you in every aspect of life. **N**othing but God can stop me standing by your side. I've got your back till the very end. You're my friend, best friend, wife and Queen. And I hope when you get this message you'll know I'm on my way to be right by your side.

Yours Sincerely,
Amos. C. Pinnock

A Little Random Thought

I actually can't be with anyone because I love too hard, care too much and would sacrifice so much just for them to be happy. I guess I have that old school kind of romantic love, because it seems like all this generation wants is sex, money, and anything they see celebrities have...

Why I'm Single

I'm not ok with being single.

I don't like it, but to me being single is a choice. Yes, I want to have the one person who symbolises the rib once taken from me, like God did to Adam in the Garden and made Eve, but I'm afraid for the other person and myself if I get into a relationship.

Not everyone can handle 100.

The rivers of affection, consideration, care and love I show will always flow, never to run dry nor leave you thirsty and seeking hydration elsewhere. We'll make a beautiful exchange where I'll put your feelings and emotions before mine and you'll put mine before yours, enabling us to understand and relate to one another. I'll place a shield of love and security over your insecurities, so you'll no longer belittle yourself but sit on the throne of unique beauty you once sat on before Instagram, the media and thoughts of others tried to make you conform and shape your image into what's fashionable in this day and age.

Clothed in confidence and maturity, you'll have no doubt in your mind that you are the one for me and there's not a soul on this earth that could divert my love and attention from you. No feelings will ever be forced, it'll all come natural like falling asleep.

Every beautiful dream will be replayed with your eyes open till the point where you wouldn't even know if you're awake or asleep.

We'll experience different levels of love, climb mountains, battle storms, conquer deserts and no situation life throws at us will bulldoze the tower of friendship and love we've built together. Day to day we'll grow stronger and deeper in love knowing that God has given us the breath of life to live another day with each other.

I don't put a limit on love, so this is why I chose to be single, and until the right time and until the right person comes, being single is a choice.

A Broken Heart

Wrong or Right

I don't know, I was just hoping to fall in love with you hopelessly every day...

...and treat every time we kiss like it's our first, hold you like we've been separated for years and treat every moment like it's our last.

Am I wrong for wanting that with you? Am I wrong for being exclusive to only you because I feel like you're oxygen to my heart? I mean, is it wrong to feel like life has a new meaning because you now exist in mine? Is it wrong to want to be in control of the hands of time, so we can stop its course so that whenever we're together goodbyes don't exist? Is it wrong to spend time on my knees praying that we experience and inherit all the happiness in the world, that each day and night you live will end with a smile?

I just want the very best for you and if giving my all too quick means you'll find the happiness and the love you're seeking, I will do it. I'm willing to put my heart on the line to ensure yours has a safe journey through life.

I hope I'm not wrong for wanting this even if you're not mine.

An Inspired Heart

Our Journey to Forever

From the moment I gazed upon your face and looked you in your eyes, my heart tried to jump out of my chest and into your hands.

At that moment, I felt like I just witnessed what it feels like to fall in love at first sight. Because emotions became an adrenalin rush to every muscle in my heart and had it beating faster than it's ever gone before.

I smiled as you smiled; I couldn't look away because in your eyes I saw heaven and that moment we shared felt like paradise. I knew from that day, it was with you I wanted to spend the rest of my life with.

I made a vow to myself and to God that no matter what, through highs and lows, I will stand by your side. I made a vow to build a fortress of love around your heart and to keep God at the centre of our relationship, because I believe and know that it was Him who had brought us together.

The more I spent time with you, the more I didn't want a day to go by where you were not in it.

Each time I saw your beautiful face, heard your sweet voice and held you in my arms, I fell deeper and deeper in love with you. And as I enjoyed falling for you, I couldn't help but fall on one knee, to ask you to marry me, for it is only you I would want my wife to be.

And now we're here, at the altar, where we'll exchange our vows and rings in the sight of God, then finally, as husband and wife, we'll share our first kiss, becoming one in the sight of God and man. It's an honour to be spending the rest of my life with the love of my life and the life of my love. I am yours. and you are mine.

Now, tomorrow, and forevermore.

10th Letter...

Dear Future Wife,

For you, my heart is a house.
    Feel free to move in and make it your home. My arms can be a seat belt, they'll protect you from whatever tries to hurt you. They'll embrace and comfort you, never letting go unless you want them to. My time a clock you can play and pause. You would never have to book me into your day because I'll be here for you 24/7.
    My efforts, always at 100%, you'll never feel like you're missing out on the profit love brings. My words, always true and given life by actions. Promises will never be broken and foul language never spoken.
    My mind, always seeking ways to make your heart overflow with love and happiness. My faith, always seeking God in prayer to be the bond that keeps us together. With no fear when hard times come, we'll come out stronger and wiser.
    And my life, I live to fulfil your hearts desires. I live to love you. So I hope you get this message so we can start a life together.

Yours Sincerely,
Amos. C. Pinnock

A Little
Random Thought

If you find someone you can have the weirdest, funniest, most serious, crazy, entertaining, heart-warming, inspiring, and life-changing conversations with, you're bound to fall madly in love with them. It's like falling in love with your best friend…

An Inspired Heart

We Reflect Each Other

You are my Lady, I am your Man. What happens between us stays between us.

I will never expose or let the world know about any problems or issues we have. If someone asks how we are doing even if we both know we're in a hard place at that moment and time, I will wear a smile and say we are great and that I love you unconditionally.

I'm not saying let's deal with our problems all by ourselves, because I know we have God, family and close friends who will support us and give us positive advice on how to deal and move forward with any problems. I'm just saying social media or ears or random people we know don't need to know about our personal life.

Yes, we may not be on the same page, but we're in the same book, and this story of our life is something I will protect and make sure that we will come to a mutual loving agreement that will have us end and create a new chapter together, on the same page, in the same mindset, learning from our mistakes and moving forward onto something better in love peace and harmony.

You are my Lady and I will protect you and our relationship from any negative tongue that tries to speak up against us. You will never be made to look like a problem or an issue. I will clothe you with words of love, kindness and beauty. Regardless of the hard times we may face, I know your intentions are never to bring me down, but are always to build me up, to encourage me and to push me to the mark of success. I promise I am here to the do the same for you.

When people see us, we represent and reflect each other.

So let's protect each other and build each other up; let's look beautiful together and stand by each other as we overcome every obstacle we face.

We are one, you are my Lady, and I am your Man, as you are mine and I am yours.

Love Out of Time

I'm dangerously in love with you.

Dangerous because you're sessional yet I place lifetime expectations on the schedule of your existence in my life.

I need to keep away from you, but your distance creates a silence I'm not used to, only causing me to want your voice to invade my ear drums, awakening emotions and making them scream and cry out for you.

Annoyed that I have to suppress my feelings because we simply can't be together, I'm lost in thought. If you're for a moment why does it feel like every moment for the rest of my life should be spent with you?

Time says I haven't known you for long enough, but my heart has been waiting for you ever since its first beat. Years of falling in love with an imagination built by my hearts desires, it was a myth to even think it could exist.

Then one day as I gazed upon you, staring into your beautiful eyes, I realised what was once an imagination in the lab of my heart is now standing in front of me. But you can't know any of this because the truth behind the words I utter could complicate us, so as I lie about concentrating on our friendship, I beg the heavens to make you a season that lasts a lifetime. I don't want you, my imagination, to disappear.

I don't want you to be a moment.

An Inspired Heart

You're My Conclusion

Visions of a future are so clear with you.

I don't know how, I don't know when, but you've been a beautiful thief and stole my heart. Without trying you captivated all my attention and had me focused on no one else but you. No need for reserves or a Plan B. No need for a "just in case" side piece; you annihilated all options and presented yourself as the one, Plan A, the tangible evidence of Genesis 2:18: *"...man should not be alone!"*

A rib taken out of me at birth and placed into the womb of your mother, our destiny had already been whispered into the ears of our souls saying *our time to be reunited will come.*

Every relationship that failed, every tear that fell, the heartache, pain and discomfort we experienced allows us to appreciate the comfort, peace and love we find in each other. Knowing that we'll share a life, with the reassuring knowledge that we're together forever, we inherit that fearless love we once craved. Finally free to love and free to be loved.

I'm yours and you're mine, forever till the end of time.

11th Letter...

Dear Future Wife,

I believe marriage is a permanent exclusive union between man and woman.

    Not only coexisting in a house together but in life, protecting each other's identity because we now are one.

    United by the powers of destiny and humbled by the arms of grace, we do not take this communion lightly. For we know there will be times when our strength will be tested, times where the light of love will seem to disappear, because sticks and stones broke the bones of our emotions and names called out of anger did hurt us, making it seem like we're in a dark place.

    But as love opens our eyes; we see we're at our bedside, knees bent, hands joined with bowed heads, offering every problem and issue to God, our concealer and guide. Asking him to educate and teach us how to sail upon stormy seas of anger, to conquer the mountains of confusion and survive the valleys of distractions. Also to teach us how to love, passionately, truthfully and honestly, giving all we have and never holding back.

    As sexually complementary spouses, we'll fulfil each other's desires, for we know sex is no longer a sinful act because we're united by the hands of God into a marriage no man can separate but Him.

    I honour and respect you, my beautiful wife, and when we seal our lives together through God, vows and rings at the altar, sacrificing our independence to a partnership, you have my word:

    I will journey with you to the end of the world, loving you with all I have to give.

Yours Sincerely,
Amos. C. Pinnock

An Inspired Heart

Vows to Love and to Care

I will be there.

Through tears and worries, through struggles, through pain, I'll never leave you alone. You'll never feel like you have no one to hold. I will carry you on my shoulders when you can't walk, I'll kneel in prayer so you can stand in faith. In our darkest hour, through times of doubt and confusion, I won't neglect you nor turn my back to you. I will still care and love, even if it hurts me to.

Take my heart as I take yours and place your hand on your chest. Now as long our hearts beat, each beat represents our love for one another. You will always have a part of me and I a part of you.

I will always be with you.

Through your trials and tribulations, in your anguish and pain, through your joy and sorrow, in the sunshine and rain, loneliness will never be your company.

These words are a declaration of my love for you and they will be given life by my actions. I'll never part nor let you part, for you are forever a part of me, and as God smiles down on us, we will lift our hearts to Him in prayer and daily renew our vows to love and to care for each other for as long as we live.

.w. I will never break this promise...

About the Author

Amos Cushi Pinnock is a young, upcoming author from Birmingham, England.

As a child Amos thoroughly enjoyed writing songs and poetry. As he grew, he lost touch with his passion for writing, moving on to pursue his love for music as a session musician. He toured Europe and performed at events that held thousands of people. Amos felt at that time, that being a session musician was all he wanted to do.

Eventually that all changed when his heart became wounded by a relationship he was committed to came to an end. Struggling to heal from the breakup, Amos found purpose in his pain. He started expressing his heart in the form of Poetry. As time went on, Amos's passion for writing grew as he felt it was a safe and perfect way to vent out his inner most feelings, instead of letting them out to the wrong person and getting hurt again.

As Amos channelled all of his pain into his writing, he was able to find the strength to heal from the breakup, but the writing never stopped there! Amos continued on his journey, but instead of writing about the pain he experienced, he wrote about love. He started with letters to his Future Wife, then he followed his heart and wrote down all that was trapped inside.

A year later, having accumulated a collection of poems and after sharing his poems with friends, family and social media, the amazing responses he received fuelled his passion and inspired him to write a book. It was later that year Amos made a commitment to find ways to share it with the world.

Amos started this book in pain and finished it through love.